Aunt Beak's Antiques
and Other Stories

By Joel A. Clark

I mean Iggy,

No luck yet.

Iggy, Iggy, Iggy, whatever will
become of you?

Aunt Beak's Antiques and Other Stories

Copyright 2012 by Joel A. Clark

ISBN-10: 0988501600

ISBN-13: 978-0-9885016-0-7

Kolozigis Publishing Company

This book is dedicated
to my dear wife,
Marnie Clark

Contents

Note: Stories are best read in sequence as some characters reappear.

Acknowledgements

I would like to thank Eric Bosarge at Eric's Hysterics,
Katherine Meehan and Graham Trail at The Ear Hustler and
the Folks at Hazard Cat for their help and encouragement.

"The Call of Duty" and "The Quantrill Gang", both by Joel A.
Clark were previously published in 2011 by The Ear Hustler, at
www.earhustlermag.com.

"Cat-O-Matic", by Joel A. Clark was previously published in
2011 by Hazard Cat, at hazardcat.blogspot.com.

"Improv Novel", by Joel A. Clark was previously published in
2011 by Eric's Hysterics, at www.erics-hysterics.com.

Cover art: acrylic painting by Joel A. Clark

Kolozigis Publishing Company

A Midnight Dreary

It was getting later and later, almost midnight. Sam needed to give something to his cranky editor right away.

"Why did I ever take this job?" lamented Sam.

"I'll whip up some poem. I haven't done a poem lately. Maybe something historical. Who was that guy who warned the minutemen around Boston? Paul something...Paul Respect? Paul Venerate?"

"Listen, my children, I shall now relate ….
The midnight ride of Paul Venerate,"

"Wait, wait, I remember now, it was <u>Revere</u>."

"Listen, my children, I'll now make clear
The story of galloping Paul Revere,"

"Better, but still not right."

"Listen, Kiddos, because I've got a little..."

"No, no."

"Keep your ears open, if you don't mind..."

"No, no, no!"

Sam closed his laptop and held his weary head in his hands. Suddenly there was a tapping at the door!

In his somber mood of despair and failure it was an ominous sound and it seemed to chill his dimly-lit chamber. Who...or what... was tapping, rapping?

Suddenly he envisioned an entire poem. Suppose he opened the door and there was nobody there! Hey, soooo spooky! Or maybe not a plain old person, but a bird!...or a plane? No, not a plane. Feverishly, Sam typed line after line.

The tapping got louder, so he opened the door. It was his pal, Joe.

"Sam, what took you so &^%^$% long to open the door?!"

"Shhh! Listen, don't say a word 'til I get this all down...it's a poem. I have to do it right away."

Joe sat scowling. A few minutes later:

"There, Joe, I've done it! The narrator is grieving and keeps seeking some glimmer of solace. But no, he can't escape his despair, represented by this inscrutable black bird...here, let

2

me read some to you..."

"Once upon a midnight dreary, while I pondered, weak and weary,"

"Wait, wait, Sam, I see what you're trying to do, but readers want something a little lighter. How's this:"

"Along about twelve-ish, Gosh, I was tired, thinking things over, you know,"

"Or maybe:"

"I looked at my watch; midnight already? I reflected on the recent tragedy,"

"No, no, no, just let me do it, Joe, it's got to keep a dark mood. Here, read the whole thing and then tell me what you think."

Joe read it, then remarked, "Apparently the unfortunate lady, Lenore, has died. But what's with the obscure girl's name? You just picked that 'cause it rhymes with door and more and stevedore.."

"No, no, there's no 'stevedore' in there!"

"And what's with the word 'nepenthe', anyway? Never in my life heard of 'nepenthe'!"

"Joe, it happens to appear in the fourth book of Homer's Odyssey (verses 220–221), as I think most people would know. It's a drug that makes you forget sorrow."

"Listen , not everybody watches "The Simpsons" y'know."

3

"Knock, knock." This time it's Sardonic Silvia, an apartment building neighbor who avoids them except when her computer bombs.

"Yes, we can help with your computer, Silvia, but first I have this poem, which I've maybe just finished. But also, we just today put together our two routines, you know, for Charlie's Vaudeville Revival, that place down the street. You can be a test audience, OK?"

"Not again!? Your Titanic skit sank like a rock like I told you, didn't it? Never mind, I'll be an audience, but then you have to get my &^%^$$% piece-of-junk computer going, OK?"

They agreed and got into their costumes. Then Sam said, "We'll run through our first one for you, Silvia:"

Cyrano de Bergerac goes into a hardware store wearing his plumed Cavalier's hat, pantaloons, and a rapier with a big handle. The clerk waits on him.

"Monsieur de Bergerac, how are you?"

"Bonsoir. I have a list of items I require. First, a horn for my bicyclette."

"Yes, we do have them, see, here is one. Simply attach it to your beak, I mean, your bike. Just tweak the bulb to blow your nose, I mean horn."

"BEAK! TWEAK! NOSE! Do you mock me, Monsieur? I will not permit the mocking!"

"No, no, goodness knows I wouldn't..."

4

"Goodness NOSE? Again this outrage, how dare you?..."

"Monsieur, let us see what is next on your shopping list... a watering can, of course. We have them. This one has a long snout allowing..."

"SNOUT, is it?, Monsieur, you play a little game? A perilous one, I assure you..."

"Wait, wait, Monsieur de Bergerac, we also have the next item on your list, a garden hose."

"Garden NOSE?? Monsieur, ..."

"No, hose, hose! We have green and we have red, take your pick. Just pick your nose, I mean hose and then you will need a shnozzle, I mean a nozzle for it..."

"SHNOZZLE!! The Shnozzle word I will not permit!"

Monsieur de Bergerac draws his rapier and brandishes it.

"En garde, Villain!"

The clerk counters with an umbrella, they parry briefly, then the clerk opens the umbrella pointed toward the baffled de Bergerac,

"Monsieur, this is not permitted!"

Then the resourceful clerk discards the umbrella and sprays de Bergerac with a hose....de Bergerac retreats, alarmed at getting his finery wet.

"Enough! Mon chapeau! Mon pantaloons! Villain, henceforth I go to Depot de Chez! Do you hear? Depot de Chez!"

"What did you think, Silvia?"

"Are you going to add jokes later? Why does Joe wear a big false nose?"

$$**********$$

"If we do this next one at the vaudeville house, we'll need a third man to play the bartender. Say, Silvia...."

"No, forget it."

"We'll get somebody. Let me read the script for this one now, Silvia:"

The skit starts with the bartender behind the Western bar. The sheriff enters and puts up a big WANTED poster.

"Luke, this here's a real desperado, he robs banks. Keep a lookout for him.

"His name's Texas Frenchie, got a patch over left eye, large handlebar mustache, wears a cartoon rabbit vest, walks like a chicken, he's left-handed and draws faster'n greased lightnin'."

6

The sheriff leaves. Then in comes a man with a grocery bag over his head with only a right eye hole. He walks like a chicken, bobbing his head forward and back as he makes jerky steps. He's got a beret on top of the bag.

"Monsieur, ze viskey, s'il vous plait."

Luke gets him the whiskey, and says:

"Ain't seen you around these parts afore, Stranger. You got business here?"

"Oui, some bank beesiness. Monsieur, do you have ze grease du axle?"

Luke brings out a can of axle grease. The stranger takes out his gun and applies some grease to his leather holster.

The sheriff comes back. The bartender gestures silently, pointing to the wanted poster, and pointing to the stranger.

The sheriff pays no attention. The suspicious man moves down the bar to get some pretzels.

Now Luke whispers to the sheriff:

"That's Texas Frenchie! See... one eye, handlebar mustache, cartoon rabbit on his vest, walks like a chicken, left-handed, got a beret and speaks French!"

The sheriff strokes his whiskers thoughtfully, but does nothing.

The stranger tosses a coin on the bar.

"Au revoir, Monsieur, merci, I must commence ze trail hitting."

The bartender, alarmed, gestures frantically to the sheriff, who does nothing. The stranger chicken-walks away.

"Sheriff, why didn't you arrest him?"

"Naw, 'tweren't him, couldn't you see? He had a squirrel cartoon on his vest, not a rabbit."

"But it was a Bugs Bunny vest!"

"Well, Bugs Bunny is a squirrel!"

"No, he ain't!"

"Well, he looks like a squirrel."

"Dad blast it! Elmer Fudd calls him a 'wascally wabbit'!"

The sheriff paused and rubbed his chin, saying:

"Oh...I guess he is a wabbit, uh, rabbit. Well, whoop-de-doo for you, Mr. Professor of Comparative Biology at Hartford University!"

"Silvia, what do you think?"

She said, "I think you need hose spraying in this one."

Sam said, "I wish I had more to send to The Blab. All I've got are two other poems. Listen, here's the first one, see what you think."

"A giant lobster from Greenwich,
Said, 'Gosh, I can't eat all this spinach',
It fell from his plate,
He grabbed, but too late."

"Good, but what's the last line?" asked Joe.

"That's all, it's a limerick, Joe. See, it has a strict form, AABB, in fact."

Joe: "Wait, no, no, it's AABBA for limericks!"

Sam: "Listen, you're thinking of that Swedish singing group..."

Silvia hasn't really been listening, but now she starts to sing "Dancing Queen".

Sam: "I'm running out of time...do you want to hear my other poem? It's called 'Mephistopheles and the Lamb'."

Joe: "How's it go?"

"Mephistopheles had a little lamb,
Its fleece was white as snow,
.............."

9

"It goes on….. school adventures, etc."

"Good, but the name, how about something like Gretchen, or Mabel, or Mary?"

"You think? I always listen to you, Joe... I'll fix it up. Tucca, tucca, ticky, tucca, ticky, tucca, ticky, tucka...There. New title: 'Mephistopheles and Mary the Lamb'."

Sam suddenly said, "My Gosh, I've got to take these poems right away to Spencer at The Weekly Blab."

Silvia said, "Well, my boyfriend, Nicky, is going right by there, I'll give it to him."

Sam printed out a copy and stuffed it in an envelope and Nicky appeared on his way out so he took it to deliver it.

Silvia said, looking at the computer screen, "Is your poem as bad as the skits? Let me see."

Then she said: "This is exactly like Poe's 'The Raven'! What are you doing?"

She read further. "Of course, many lines are different, such as your line:"

"The phone rang just then, is it Lenore? No, wait, she's dead!"

"And of, course your title, 'The Turkey' is different, or is that referring to the author? But you'll surely get fired for gross plagiarism, too bad."

10

"Silvia, ...plagiarism? What?? I've got to get it back!!"

"Well, good luck, Nicky's pretty fast with that motor scooter."

Sam ran down the stairs and out to the street. He frantically hailed a taxi. Nicky was not too far ahead.

"Quick, follow that white Vespa!"

"Who the Heck are you, Columbo?"

Marina Days

It was late in the day by the time I walked to Bev's place. A charitable description would be "ramshackle dump of a house". On stilts, mostly. Surrounded by swamp hummocks. Sign said, "Beak Bay Marina and Restaurant".

At eighteen, I'd had enough farming and I just took off for warmer places. Don't ask me why, but I arrived on the Louisiana coast, a swampy part. Well, I'll tell you why, I'd been studying the photographs in a Chris-Craft catalog and there was no shortage of good-looking girls admiring the lads who tooled around and about in their mahogany power boats.

I'd been warned that this person Bev was possibly too flaky to run a business, so I didn't know what to expect.

I went around to the marina side. Twenty or thirty boats, all sizes, narrow floating docks all over. And just crowded with people? What a popular place! No, when I blinked, I could see dozens of wooden full-sized people cutouts, like those movie lobby cutouts, but these were apparently weatherproofed.

I saw Bev. She didn't look like a grouchy old lady business owner, as you might expect. No, it was an elegant <u>young</u> lady with light brown hair that framed her radiant good looks, eyes bright and smiling. Well, she had a few years on me, if you want to know, but I knew immediately that I wanted to stick around there.

She was at an outdoor table having a coffee and playing Klondike solitaire beside a seated wooden cutout. A Western character. Table strewn with artist's brushes and paints.

"Oh ho!" she said, finally seeing me. "Howdy, didn't hear you at first, Hon. Don't sneak up on my friend here, Wild Bill Hickok, he gets nervous sometimes."

Wild Bill was holding a poker hand close to his chest. (That squint made him look more like Popeye without the pipe, but I don't wish to be critical.)

"Hello, Ma'am," I said. "Beautiful day, isn't it?"

"Oh, I'm not Ma'am," she sighed. "I'm Bev. This is Billy, as I said. A good companion, a bit taciturn, though. He was fading, so I'm giving him a touch-up this morning. He said, 'Maybe I ain't the only one who's fading.'. I put crumbs in his moustache, just for that."

Bev said, sure, she could use some help, she had no employees, did the cooking and everything herself. But she had no money to hire anybody, the business was just about kaput.

14

She had only two paying customers for the slip rentals. The rest of the boats were all inoperable and considered junk by insurance companies and couldn't be licensed, but made the marina look full. Hurricanes provided plenty of them.

"Henry, you can hang around and help, but I can't pay yet, maybe never. You could learn the marina business, no, wait,.... I don't know the marina business myself."

"Where you stayin'?" she continued.

"Nowhere, yet."

"You can stay in one of those cabin cruiser hulks, I guess, see that one? If it sinks and you drown, don't blame me. I'm haunted already... by swamp ghosts. Plus the ghost of the former owner of this dump, Capt. Dutcher. He's scary, the old coot. Discovered Spanish wrecks with gold. Thinks I'm after his treasure, 'course I would be if I knew where to look."

****

There was plenty to do, pumping out leaky boats, scraping and painting topsides. A short walk along the shore from us was a little beach and dock. I had a gander, now and then. Was I watching for girls? Yes. And one, two, three materialized. Not only that but after swimming awhile one of them came this way along the shore path.

A beauty to behold, just like one of the girls in the Chris-Craft catalog pages I examined a few hundred times. Light brown hair, wet now from swimming.

I'm busy with my important work. I pretend I haven't been

watching her every girlish, carefree step. One-piece light blue bathing suit, cotton man's shirt over her shoulders.

"Hi, do you work here?" she said.

"YES..yeah ..," I conversed, wittily.

The silky voice continued, "I'm new around here and my girl friends and I saw your place. Do you rent boats? I mean, for water skiing, maybe?"

"We do rent water...uh..," I pointed to Bev. "If you ask that leggy,....I mean, lady..."

"OK, thanks."

She talked briefly with Bev, and went back to the beach.

Ever so casually, I inquired, "By the way, Bev, that girl who just came by. Any idea where she's from? Around here?"

"So you're throwing me over for a young chick? And here I've been expecting an engagement ring any day now."

"Any man would be a fool not to offer you one, Bev," I said, gallantly. "My boss would have to pay me enough to buy something like that."

"Your boss has no money. I guess I'll have to keep waiting for a prince, or, second choice, a tramp.

"That girl was Ginny Albemarle, I know her father because I've got some boats in his warehouse.

"Look, if you're not going to propose to me right now, let's talk about something else. It's good news. These cutouts I made …a restaurant owner saw them and wants to know if he can buy some like them, so I said, 'Sure'."

The amazing Beverly had a large band saw in a back room and plenty of marine plywood on hand. We set about making the cutouts. I particularly liked making the shapely females, for some reason.

She painted, I painted, and, best of all, Ginny, who must have good vision, saw from the beach what we were painting and wanted to help. She was much better than either of us. A casual observer would think Abraham Lincoln and Napoleon had stopped by the Beak Bay Restaurant for a snack.

Dear Reader, a cascade of good fortune came forth. Bev offered to hire Ginny if we got more orders! Also, the painting led to discussion of stage scenery, and theater generally, and I was able to modestly relate my high school play career of two roles, Palace Guard (With Halberd), and Assassin No. 2.

Thirdly, there was a summer theater project in the planning stages she and her pals were working on, to be staged at the local yacht club. Could involvement by Yours Truly be somehow wangled? We shall see, thought I.

****

There was an open-cockpit powerboat at one end of the dock area that dwarfed any other she had. Over 30 feet long. "La Bamba" on the stern in faded letters.

"It's just a derelict boat I bought. The engine doesn't run, but might be fixable," Bev said.

"That baby could be a nice tourist attraction," I said.

"How? It's just a big speedboat."

I held up my hand. "In time it shall be revealed," I said.

A couple of days later I had it labeled with a big sign: "Fidel Castro's Getaway Boat". And I had painted it with seagoing camouflage.

I made a glass case in the dining room telling the elaborate and fictitious story of how right outside we have the fast boat Castro kept secretly at the ready to escape from enemies if he needed to. Hurricane Alphonse tore it loose, and carried it to the nearby coastal waters. President Kennedy was not about to return it to a hostile dictator. It is not at some museum, but at this very facility, Beak Bay Marina and Restaurant. Also there were photos of the seven million in U.S. Currency found in a cash box aboard it!

"What do you think, Boss? Nice thing is, how could you check it? You'd expect Cuba to deny it since it's embarrassing. You could charge more to rent Castro's personal secret getaway boat."

"I like it, SuperHenry!" said Bev.

"No, no, I'm not SuperHenry," I protested. "But I do have his cell phone number."

Ginny stopped by on a sunny Wednesday.

"We'd love to take that one out, or you could drive and we could water ski."

"Castro's Getaway Boat? Trouble is, the engine doesn't run," I sighed.

"Look, my dad has a warehouse business, and he could send over one of the mechanics to take a look at it. How 'bout that?"

She phoned and pretty soon a truck rumbled up and a young, handsome guy appeared with a toolbox. I hated him before he got out of his truck. He had bulging arm muscles from tightening countless engine bolts. I hated him more the closer he got. Why couldn't they send over a geezer with a pot belly?

His name was Greg something. Greg Palooka, probably.

He stood around talking to my Ginny, "Your father is a great guy, blah, blah." Just fix the %%$#^^ boat, Mr. Palooka.

Ginny went back to swim with her girl pals and I pumped bilges on some of the old tubs. Couple hours later I heard the roar of the huge engine. The girls came running and Mr. Hero Mechanic took them and Bev for an unnecessary "test spin".

The guy finally left, and I could stop grinding my teeth.

But Bev set things up beautifully, bless her heart. "Ginny, we really want to thank you and your dad. This boat isn't licensed yet so we can't rent it out, but Henry can give you a ride tomorrow, just not long, 'cause we'll get fined if the Coast Guard nabs us."

****

I spent the evening cleaning and spiffing up the fake Castro boat. I was up early in the morning and made myself some coffee. Bev not around yet. It was part of the deal, I worked for no pay, but at least got food and a place to stay.

I sat down beside the Helen of Troy cutout and sipped the hot brew. "Ms. Troy, you look beautiful this morning! How do you do it? How about some coffee?" She nodded, her sly smile somewhat fixed, "Sure, thanks. Long time since I had a cup, 3,000 years, maybe. A Mediterranean blend, I hope?"

We lingered awhile, enjoying our coffees, then I said, "Later, Babe." She likes it if you're a little fresh. Did she wink or was it just a glint of sunlight?

The girls showed up, with water skis. We piled in, I threw off the lines and started the big engine. I carefully maneuvered to open water. "We'd better tow one skier at a time, to see how the boat handles," I said authoritatively.

The engine quit. I tried starting it, but it just went, "Rrrrrr rrrrr rrrr." I remembered the mechanic talking about the throttle linkage; it was one thing he fixed. Maybe it came loose. I got up on the deck and pulled open the big engine hatch. Maybe did it wrong 'cause I fell over backwards into the water. "SPLAAASHHH!"

I went kind of deep and was heavy with clothes and shoes. I floundered my way to the surface. I suppose being underwater spared me hearing some guffaws. "Hope you're OK, Henry." They helped me get in again. They had a good time laughing, I must say.

Trixie said, "Henry, would you do that again, I didn't see it."
"Ha, ha, hee, hee!"

Laura said, "Henry, maybe you'd better not try to fix the engine; maybe you're in over your head." "Ha, ha, hee,hee."

Very funny, girls. Luckily, it was just an empty gas tank and we got in some skiing runs. Bev waved us back, fearing the gendarmes might be about.

****

The cutouts business boomed. Bev began to pay me modestly. I got top quality clothes from the Salvation Army Store.

I felt the theater thing was my big opening, the way to win dear Ginny's heart. Maybe they hadn't decided what thing to do at the club. Well, instead of some tired Oscar Wilde trifle, how about an original work with maybe a local setting. Got to hurry, though. I was thinking, thinking, while I finished a pile of cutouts. Covered with sawdust, I hurried to find Bev to borrow some paper and pencils.

Yes, she had some. "Going to write a play for Ginny?" she asked.

"Gaak! Can you read my mind?" I gasped.

"Yes, Ducky."

I found a quiet spot in the dining room and looked at the blank paper. Let's see, who'll be the star? Ginny. Something up-lifting, ahh, she's singing…

21

It'll be a musical! Joyous songs, enthusiasms, she'll be in love with life, and…

Wait, I have no knowledge of music. What am I doing? What kind of fool am I? Oh no, that's a song title. They've all been written by now.

I got up and made some coffee.

I'll call it "The Golden Days of Summer". It'll be a metaphor for life, full of activity, strife, conflict, resolution and all too soon, sadly ending.. Summer always ends, so does life, sniff.

Do the end, the last song:

A bunch of verses, then the last being:

Long sha/dows on/ the lawn,
All sum/mer friends/ have gone,
Stage cur/tain's be/ing drawn,

Then the refrain:

It's just/ the sad/dest time/ of all,
When gol/den days/ of sum/mer fade/ to fall.

They'll cry in the aisles! A two-hankie finish!

Now, what other songs? Well, what's the plot?

Lovable and carefree wanderer arrives at broken-down failing seaside restaurant and woos gorgeous girl who frequents swimming area. Rival mechanic impresses girl, but is shown to be cowardly when black bear appears, wanderer saves the day by batting the bear with his mandolin.

A subplot involves the lonesome beautiful former actress, career faded, owes money, will lose all to bank. Troubadour, also expert golfer, uses all unoccupied floating docks to make floating golf greens and tees, a landless course, small at first, then complete eighteen holes, water-going golf carts taken between tee and green, new successful business, it's franchised since the troubadour also is a former corporate lawyer who knows all about franchising.

The beach girl, foolish and callow, still likes the bumbling, cowardly idiot mechanic who collects hubcaps, but then she catches him stealing hubcaps from her father's antique auto. In a rage, evil mechanic tries to run her down with motorcycle. Troubadour, stronger than he looks, heaves both mechanic and motorcycle into the canal and wins the girl!

Now for some song titles, I'll slap in some content later:
"The Sparkle in Your Eyes", "Sea Spray", "We Regret We Must Foreclose", "Speed is my Name", "Castle in the Sand", "Golden Days", "Looking Far Away", "Moving Shadows", "On the Green", "Just Watchin' Waves", "A Little Wiser Now", "Raindrops On The Water", "Laugh With Me".

I worked on it every evening, thinking about it during the day. Four days later it was done. Of course, Bev had snooped often and kibitzed. I told her: "Don't blab a word to Ginny."

Now I was ready to show it to Ginny. I practiced how I would broach the subject.

"Oh, by the way, I happen to have written this play, a musical, really, and why don't you drop your previous plans and use my musical?"

"You know, it's an interesting coincidence. I wrote a play, oh, years ago, and I found it again, and...."

But it's too forward for me to write a play for her. Just get it accepted, after it's a success, I can modestly confess I wrote it.

"Say, I found this script on a park bench, and...."

"One time I copied in longhand, an entire play written by George S. Kaufman, sure to be a winner, a play by him, maybe you'd...."

"Ginny, Bev wrote this play, imagine that, and she's too shy to offer it to you..."

Ginny came over around noon.

"Henry, I'm so happy!" she said. "Greg Grublander wrote a musical for us!"

"Gasp," I remarked.

"You know that hunky guy that fixed the engine? He's a writer and an actor, too."

"That's incredible," I said. I didn't mean incredible, great, I meant incredible that a Neanderthal could read and write.

Bev heard the talking and came outside where we were. Ginny showed us the script. Her dad had gotten his office to make up bound copies.

"It's called 'Axle Grease'. Lots of action and great songs."

She enthused in some detail which I can't bear to relate. I'll summarize: Ex-con auto mechanic wins motorcycle race and the girl, beating up rivals along the way.

Examples of songs: "You Mah Babe, Babe!", "Burnin' Rubber!", "Show Me the Money, Honey!", "I Smell a Rat!", "See This Fist?", "Don't Monkey With My Heart".

"I'm going to be the girl, Betty Lou, and Greg has agreed to play the lead, Slade."

Bev, kindly soul that she was, nodded and expressed approval at these dismal revelations.

I could only stare and blink. Dear Reader, could it get any worse than this? Yes, it could.

"Are you OK, Henry? You know, we thought of you, too. Would you like to play a part? The professor. The professor comes in the garage to get his bicycle fixed. You'd sing 'Do You Have Bicycle Air?'. Cute song."

I heard myself saying, "Ginny, I'd love to."

"Great, I gotta go now. Here's the music, you can practice. Rehearsal in a couple of days. I've gotta go sing with Greg after he gets done at the garage. Bye."

Presently, as I stared stonily out to sea, Bev asked, "You didn't offer your script?"

"Too late, now. Don't tell anybody about my script, you promised. It would just make things worse."

"Henry, you wrote a great script, especially the places where you took my advice. But...what's with the description, 'fading former actress'? Oh my...if you do go shopping for diamonds, better be a pretty big one."

****

"Henry, good news. I talked to some town bigwigs about your idea for the floating golf course! You know, from your musical! They love it!"

"Bev, that was just a plot gimmick, for comic relief."

The crazy, amazing Beverly continued, "Henry, listen to these names and tell me what you think: Landless Golf, Water Golf, Floating Golf Course, Hawaiian Golf, we need a good name, see?"

"Bev, Bev, Bev..... whatever will become of you? It was just a musical play."

"Maybe we're IN a musical!" Bev assumed an Ethel Merman pose. "What song should I sing? How about 'In the Good Old Summertime'? How about a duet?"

She had queried the town to see if she could place a collection of island greens plus island tees and even island sand traps out in the harbor. Of course they all said no immediately because that's what town officials always do.

But... Bev is beautiful and charming and all the town board

members are men. They let her keep talking and they thought twice about it. No actual real estate required, just rafts with turf! Doesn't obstruct boat traffic, it's just like moored boats, harbors are full of them.

One of the board members was a real estate tycoon and made a deal to partner with Bev and build one hole as a test extending from her marina, and the guy didn't fool around. Construction people showed up and in two weeks it was ready to go!

Pretty simple really, just rafts with turf on them, some sloping on the green, boats to take the place of golf carts. Plus floating golf balls to avoid losing too many.

The town guys were hitting shots before they even finished construction and everybody seemed happy. Bev invited Ginny and any of her friends, too, and they would be coming the next day.

****

I don't want to puff myself, but I played some golf in high school. After the town people left, I thought I'd take a few shots, get ready for tomorrow.

"THWACK!" Dropped it on the green about 100 yards away. Several more, same thing. "Hah," I thought, "I haven't forgotten how to hit."

The next day, the darlings Ginny, Trixie, and Laura appeared at about noon.

"I've only hit balls at a driving range a couple of times," said Ginny.

The other girls had never even done that, but wanted to give it a try.

I had a vision of me with my powerful arms around Ginny. "Let me position your arms for the address," I'd say.

Bev was busy with customers. I said, "I'll show you the set-up, but then I have work to do, and you can handle it all yourselves."

"Here's the tee, hit from here to the green over there, then take this outboard and go and putt out."

Trixie tried a few hits. Bloopers. Laura, same thing. Laura said, "Henry, are you a golfer? You try."

"OK," I said. I coolly took a few practice swings, then addressed the ball. Drew back slowly, downswing, "SWISH" Missed completely.

"Hmm, lost my balance there."

Carefully set up again. Topped the ball. It dribbled into the water. Many giggles. Why is it that girls, who are maybe eighteen or more, still giggle?

"OK. I'm just not used to the way this raft moves, y'know. One more."

"Yesterday I was hitting them fine," I said, lamely.

Third try. Way under it, popped it up and everybody ducked. I stumbled backwards and dropped my club and it bounced into the water.

Just then, Ginny said, "Hey, it's Greg! C'mon over. I thought you had to work. We're trying the new golf game."

Many greetings. It was Greg's day off. How wonderful. Every-body was glad to see Greg. Well, not everybody was glad.

"Looks like fun, Ladies, who's turn?" asked Greg Muscles.

"You go, Greg," said Ginny.

Greg found a club. "Do we have the yardage? Looks to be 100."

No practice swing. "THWACK!" Right on the green, pin high. "Missed a little, this raft moves, don't it?"

"Wowie, show us how to do that, Greg!" said Ginny.

****

"Knock, knock, knock." I woke up, with a start. Bev was knocking at my boat cabin door. Insisting she was not the least bit afraid of ghosts, she suggested we have a little 2:00 AM game of gin rummy and coffee.

As our game proceeded, she told me more. It was the pesky Capt. Dutcher. "He is trying to tell me something," she said. "You know my bedroom was his room, also he died in that room. If a ghost were returning, maybe that's where he'd show up.

"I felt a cold hand on my shoulder, Henry! I woke up screaming! Of course, I don't believe there are ghosts, it's nonsense."

The next morning, Bev said, "I don't want us to worry about ghosts. I'm going to call Ms. Strattenbatten, who is well known as a medium around here. We'll hold a séance, and if this old grouchy ship captain wants to say something, we'll help him make a connection. What do you think?"

"Bev, these mediums are all frauds who suck money from gullible..."

"Good, I thought you'd agree. I'll set it up. We'll use that little room off the dining room."

Later, I was busy painting a Mona Lisa cutout. "She's not smiling," said Kibitzer-In-Chief.

"Yes, she is, she's just being coy."

"Hmmm, so coy she'll be an old maid," said Bev, "Listen, the séance is set for tonight at midnight. Want to sit in?"

"Bev, it's a waste of time..."

"Ginny and Trixie will be there..."

"....but sure, why not?" I said.

Midnight. We were assembled in the little very dark room in Bev's big old spooky house/restaurant. The air was heavy with anticipation. Some were thinking about ghosts. I was thinking about holding hands with Ginny, Trixie, or Bev.

Ms. S. started us off in a quiet voice with some claptrap about the spirit world and how it filled her with joy to have the "gift" of being a channel for messages from the dearly departed. She didn't mention the joy of getting money for babbling nonsense.

Once she went into her trance, we must all focus intently upon her and the ethereal beings struggling to speak to us, and not let our minds wander.

"Captain Frederick G. Dutcher, picture this man, all of you!" She related some details and description to assist us, so we would not be pulling in some other gnarly sea captain by mistake.

"At 4:25AM February 17, 1930, Captain Dutcher passed to the other side from this very house."

"Aaaaaahhhh......aaaaaaaaaaahhhh....." Ms. S. commenced a lengthy monologue of sounds. I surmised she was either trying to cure a case of hiccups, or going into a trance.

It was a trance. In a low voice she repeated the old sea dog's name over and over, sort of like a P.A. system call at Grand Central Station. Then without even an "Over, Good Buddy", we heard a gravelly, old man's voice.

Who could it be? Who or what was it? I believe all present were hoping it was the disembodied spirit of Captain Dutcher, at long last able to express his urgent thoughts to us, who were still mucking about on this side.

It was!

Dear Reader, historical accounts pegged the captain as stern and taciturn. It seems his untimely transition in 1930 was not merely from living to dead, but from tight-lipped grouch to loquacious Rotarian!

The good Captain seemed full of good wishes for all his relatives, including his "grand niece" Beverly, who wasn't related at all. She bought the place from strangers a few years back. Of course such a mistake was understandable because of the advanced age of the old fellow, or it could be understandable because Ms. S. goofed up.

As much as I enjoy hearing news from exotic locales, I must admit I was somewhat disappointed. Apparently holding hands around the table was not part of Ms. S.'s modus operandi, so no cheap thrills there.

I may have nodded off for some of the exciting communications, but I do remember this part: Dutcher had requested his wife's gold locket be buried with him. It wasn't, because he had mistakenly buried it with a huge chest of gold coins he had recovered from many Spanish wrecks.

If it wasn't too much trouble, he said, please dig up the box, find the gold locket and stuff it in with his remains. Then he could at last rest and stop haunting Bev or others. And where to dig, pray tell? If he remembered right, at a nearby sandy beach (easy digging there), with a dock next to it.

Right about then the spooky communications tailed off, with nary a goodbye. Dead quiet, except for a little whistle of wind in the trees outside in the inky blackness.

Bev thanked Ms. S. and she left. Bev made some coffee and the four of us sat for a bit to clear our heads.

"You were right, Henry, a transparent fake," Bev said, stirring her coffee. "Say, why don't we play some cards for awhile?"

We got out the cards and Bev brought some chocolate chip cookies.

"It's not that I'm afraid to be alone or anything, ha, ha, ha. This ghost stuff is nonsense."

In the next few days there was a rash of mysterious excavations in the public beach area and even near Bev's docks. It didn't take Sherlock Holmes to suspect our recent séance had been discussed here and there. The beach looked like a war zone. The town closed and roped off the pock-marked area, but people still came at night with flashlights, dodging the periodic patrol cars.

On a fine Thursday morning I walked into town and bought some sticky coffee buns that I knew Bev liked. The Beak Bay restaurant was open but there were no customers, so we sat for awhile having a coffee.

"Y'know, Bev, there are no more orders for the cutouts, so Ginny won't be coming to paint any," I said (whined). "The girls won't be coming to the closed beach. But at least I'll see Ginny at rehearsals for that depressing production at the club."

Bev sipped her coffee. Then: "By the way, if you decide to come to your senses and come back to me, remember girls like a pretty big diamond, but not ostentatious, y'know. And not from a pawn shop, please, no previously engraved name, it's a giveaway."

A couple of days later, Trixie and Ginny came over to see if Bev had some clothes they could borrow for the theater production. From the front deck we heard beautiful music. Bev happened to be playing Beak Bay's old piano, which she often did, and singing, too. Not for diners, there weren't any, which was often the case, sad to say.

Guess what! It was a song from my never-to-be-produced musical (don't cry now):

"The sands/ were white/ and warm,
Sometimes/ a thund/erstorm,
Sandpip/ers by/ the swarm,
It's just/ the sad/dest time/ of all,
When gol/den days/ of sum/mer fade/ to fall."

"Where is that from? What a sappy song!" said Ginny. "Don't tell her I said that, OK?"

"Where do you suppose she got that hokey thing from?" asked Trixie.

"Good question, ha, ha, ha," I said. In my head, I chanted, "Don't tell them, Bev, Don't tell them, Don't tell them!"

Later, I came to the club in town for the second rehearsal of my humiliating role as the clueless professor. Ginny, always with an endearing smile, brushed wisps of silken hair from her classic face, and apologetically told me the yacht club had a limited time slot for the show, so they had to shorten it and my part was cut. Sorry.

"Oh, I understand," I said, heroically concealing my dashed hopes and broken heart.

"It's really too bad, it was a great gag where they tell you you need front tire air for the front and rear tire air for the rear! Hee, hee, hee."

Perhaps feeling a bit guilty for chucking even my tiny role overboard, she offered to give me the bent-wheeled bike, since they didn't need it now. The wheels were pear-shaped, they still turned, but you couldn't ride it. The tires were ballooned out in spots. As you pushed it along it bobbed up and down like a rocking horse toy. Of course, I graciously accepted, as though I had always wanted a clown bike.

****

Two suits in dark glasses appeared one morning at the Beak Bay. Bev was waiting on some restaurant customers and I was pumping one of the many leaky "pretend customer" boats.

"We're from the FBI, Ma'am," one said.

Somehow they had heard about the Castro's Getaway Boat gimmick. They inspected my P.T. Barnum handiwork in the glass case while Bev and I stood around. I thought, "Oh no, they think we have the money and they want to confiscate it!"

"What makes you folks think this boat was Castro's?"

I piped up, "Sir, this is just a gimmick, it's not Castro's boat. I made up a story to add a little local color to the Beak Bay Restaurant. Heh, heh."

"Heh, heh," said Agent No. 1, with a non-laugh.

"What research did you do to get all these facts you wrote about here?"

"Sir, there are no facts, it's all made up stuff."

The two agents moved away from us and talked between themselves. They made cell phone calls.

"We've got a little problem, Folks. First off, everything I'm going to tell you now we'll deny we ever said. Got it?"

In a lower voice, he continued, "The fact is, Castro DID have a getaway boat, a U.S. Navy SEAL team stole it and the whole thing has been kept secret. You, Sir, could be accused of disclosing secrets, with dire penalties involved."

"On the other hand, if you were arrested and so on, we'd have trouble keeping a lid on things. We're going to take this display and that 'Castro's Boat' sign and destroy them."

"My advice to you, Sir, before any other government people come around asking where you obtained these secrets that you disclosed, is to get in that boat and speed far away from here. This will be good for you and will save us a lot of paperwork."

"And in the future, say, 'No, I've never been to Louisiana'."

They left, taking the display and sign.

I looked at Bev and said, "Yikes!"

Then I said, "Ilsa...."

I started again, "Ilsa...Ilsa, I'm sorry, I can't remember any lines from 'Casablanca'."

I gave Bev a hug, and quickly stashed my worldly possessions in the boat, the largest of which was a certain clown bicycle.

"I'll write to tell you where to retrieve the boat, after I ditch it," I said.

Dear Bev said, "Does this mean no diamond ring? Even a small diamond might do. Oh well, I know you'll come back."

I started the noisy engine and left the dock, waving goodbye as I made waves across the harbor in Castro's Getaway Boat.

****

Hours later I settled the bow on a sandy shore and tied the boat to be sure it wouldn't float away. It was a long narrow beach. I was getting ready to stretch out on a soft spot to sleep for the night.

Then I saw a figure in the distance, coming closer. It was a girl. It was my Ginny! She had followed me....she heard of my leaving...she was broken-hearted.....now she's closer....

Wait, it's not Ginny, her hair is different, but, wow, so good-looking, am I dreaming?

"Hi, I saw your huge powerboat and I had to come see it. I love these open inboard boats! Chris-Craft used to make them. They don't make them like this anymore."

She walked around the sleek inboard.

"Where'd you ever get it, it's beautiful!?"

"Ha, ha, it has quite a history."

She was still wet from swimming, her bare feet sandy. She smoothed her hair and she leaned a little forward, closer to me, teasing me with her light blue smiling eyes.

"You could offer me a ride....Mr....uhh..."

"I'm Henry. Sure, let's go. It's not mine. I have to return it, but not, you know, immediately."

Newspaper Days

The freight train came clattering into Mushville about 1:00 AM. I'd come across three states (I ain't telling which) and I was dog-tired. I hopped off the boxcar on the dark side.

Big cop was standing there.

"Are you Texas Slim?"

"No."

"Are you Hobo Pete?"

"No."

"Gonna keep me guessin'?"

"Officer, how'd you know I was on this freight car?"

"Detectors, Dummy, you can't go riding freight cars no more.

A rube, aintcha?"

Then he said, "Let me guess once more. Dusty Ringley?"

"How'd you know?"

"Hah!, Ringy-Dingy, I know Mr. Harding at the paper, he said you'd be comin'. So I figured maybe the live body on car 578 was you. We ain't all hicks out here."

The next day Mr. Harding, Editor-in-Chief of The Daily Klaxon, started me on police blotters and a list of people to interview. I headed out to cover my beat. Mushville will keep no secrets from me!

I headed to the Second Precinct. The Duty Sergeant let me see the blotter. It was empty. "Slow news day," I remarked. "Most of 'em are, I'm glad to say," says the Sarge.

Coming out I bumped into my cop friend from the railroad tracks.

"Not much news today, Ringley, but c'mon, I'll buy you a coffee. I'll give you a ride, but keep it quiet, against regs, y'know. If I get a call, I'll have to ditch you, it'll be serious police business, then.

"Sure wish we worked in twos, I'd have somebody to talk to. Say, I didn't know what to do about my gun, had, like a sticky trigger. I really pictured a bad scene, y'know a gunman throws down on me, I react quick, but can't fire because of the trigger pull bein' hard. Ulp! Sayonara, brave Officer Spence...you'd have a write-up for your pulp fiction newspaper."

We wheeled a hard left, did about sixty for a couple of blocks.

"So, I feel better now, I filed it just a little, not a hair trigger, just nice and light, no fear left now in Officer Spence's heart."

But more fear in Newspaperman Ringley's heart. I tried to think of a polite way to call him a reckless idiot, just then a call came in:

"BxxP...Car 4, a 34 in progress, Tony's Coffee Shop...Bxxp"

He didn't ditch me. About ten seconds later, we pulled into Tony's, siren blaring. What's a 34? Armed robbery? Murders happening?

Spence can move! Blasts through the door, customers flatten against the walls and duck behind tables.

I guess a 34 is suspicious sounds from a dumpster. That's what Louise reports.

"You all stay here." He went out back. Of course, we all followed to see the shootout.

"This is the police! You out back here, show yourself with your hands up!"

Another noise from the dumpster, and Officer Spence slaps leather and "BANG!" That was the shot. "WHIRRRAAA-ANNNG!" That was the ricochet. Big dent in the dumpster.

"%&^%$$! Didn't mean t'shoot!" he said, then, "OK, Come out, and make it quick!"

Nobody appeared. No sounds.

"Everybody back inside, whoever it is, he's ignoring a police order, a hard case and dangerous. I'll need some backup."

The backup soon came and, seeing he was surrounded by four of Mushville's finest, the raccoon in the dumpster gave up.

"Ringley, you can't report this for the paper, y'know."

"But it was a police call and with a backup, too. A 34."

"%^$$#&, it was just a raccoon, not a crime, you can't report that."

"Wait, didn't that raccoon commit a crime? Breaking and entering? Had kind of a mask, too, suspicious right there!

"Hey, just kidding, Spence, I won't write it up, even though I'm desperate for news."

****

H.L. Mencken got his start newspapering, and a passel of other writers did, but maybe I won't. It can have boring days. So far, every day.

I was talking to some Future Hack Writers of America at the library writer's group:

"My editor, Mr. Harding, has to fill up a daily in this no-news town, so he prints everything. Stringers send in their cousin's vacation news, there's the deer-in-a-yard story, a cat-up-a-tree story, Cuthbert Pixley-enlisted-in-the-National Guard story.

"It's so boring, I'm quitting for sure, soon's I get a few bucks together for transportation."

There was some discussion about why we wanted to be writers.

Heather gave her answer:

"I wrote a story in high school about a hobo who dressed in a neat suit and tie and was able to crash company picnics by just showing up and pretending to know people. It was good for some fine food and he would stuff his plastic-lined pockets, too. He met a gorgeous girl and she took a shine to him, but soon the party was over and he was on another freight car.

"The other tramps asked why he brushed away a tear. Then he goes to the next boxcar in line and sees the same girl in a fine dress who was also crashing the party and she takes his hand in hers. My teacher was an old maid and she was in tears when she gave it back to me. That's when I knew I wanted to write things."

This was met with general approval.

I piped up and said, "Funny, when I was in high school, I wrote exactly the same story, except the girl was an FBI agent and she arrested him for theft and for being in a high security area and he got three years in the pen."

Heather said, "Very funny, Mr. Smart Aleck."

Some of the group read stuff they were working on.

Maudie started reading her boring, stupid story about a guy

who comes to a hick town on a freight train, cop surprises him as he gets off, asks if he's Texas Slim or Hobo Pete...

"I've got it!" I interrupted. "Listen, there's five of us. Just enough for my plan." I quietly closed the door to the library conference room. "Before I say another word, everybody put your right hand on this Bible (actually, Cliff Notes Bible) and swear you won't tell anybody my, our, plan."

Everybody loves a conspiracy, so I sucked them all in. All you have to do is whisper.

In a nutshell, my plan was to report outlandish stuff and see if there was any limit to what my boss Mr. Harding would print!

There were a bunch of ideas, they were supposed to be writers, after all. We picked "SPACE ALIENS LAND!" for our first bamboozle.

I said, "We need an out-of town person willing to dress up as a clergyman." There were several names suggested. Who do we know that might believe National Enquirer type stories? Ellie Jarvis's name popped up. Good, they have a farm.

I outlined how we would do it and how next week we'd do another scheme.

"I'll get Spence to help. See you next week."

Everybody was leaving. "But I didn't finish my story..." Maudie said.

"Next meeting you can finish..... oh, OK, whisper to me more of it."

She continued her lame tale…was it supposed to be funny or what? It was dragging, so I rudely said, "Sorry I have to go…we'll listen next time." She gave me a downcast look.

"Maudie, what happens at the end?"

"Whisper, whisper, whisper.."

"Oh, three caballeros endings are trite…may I suggest a better ending?" I said.

I continued, "Whisper, whisper, whisper… Yeah, Maudie, that's what I'd do. Whatever you do, don't end with three guys singing that stupid song! See you next week!"

I easily enlisted Spence's help. Simple plan: The out-of-town hoaxer will dress as the fictitious Reverend McPherson. His 12-yr-old son will be the green alien (costume from distant shop). The storyline: Spaceship lands in cornfield near National Enquirer-reading Ellie's place. Rev. McPherson happens along on his bike and meets the alien emerging from the flying saucer. The news stringer just happens to be driving along and photographs this meeting. It's dark. Space ship is really pie plate photos Photoshopped into background. Spence and I stomp down a cornfield "landing area".

Mr. Harding's news stringer Dan reported the amazing events . the next day.

The Wednesday edition of The Daily Klaxon told the tale with a headline:

GREEN SPACE ALIEN LANDS IN MUSHVILLE,

ABDUCTION SUSPECTED!

"It was definitely a real alien," said Ms. Ellie Jarvis of this city, who opened her door Tuesday about 9:15 PM to greet the Reverend McPherson and the alien. "Funny, I wasn't scared, well, the Reverend was there and so it seemed the little green man was not dangerous."

Ms. Jarvis reports that McPherson introduced himself and his green, four-foot-tall companion, saying he had been bicycling along and this huge flying saucer landed in the Jarvis's cornfield. He then met the strange creature and talked to him through sign language. He thought he wanted some water, so Ms. Jarvis got him a glass. "I called to Jethro, but he thought it was just a normal tramp that sometimes show up, and didn't come right away."

When interviewed, Mr. Jarvis expressed regret that he missed seeing the extraterrestrial, which appears to be a first in the history of mankind, but he was watching an exciting TV program at the time and didn't come quickly because seeing a tramp didn't seem very important. Ms. Jarvis said, "He was watching that stupid show 'TV Babes'!"

*The alien took the glass of water and poured it into an opening in the **top of his** head. Then the little guy seemed agitated and headed off into the darkness, along with McPherson.*

Our reporter, Dan Gregory, had earlier luckily happened to be driving by and photographed the meeting of the alien and the Reverend which is seen here in our report. We apologize for the blurring due to camera motion.

After taking the photograph, Mr. Gregory examined the

46

*spacecraft for awhile, then proceeded to the Jarvis's only to find they had left already, and when he returned to the site of the spaceship it was **gone and there was no sign of Reverend McPherson**!*

His bicycle was still there. It's possible he was invited or forced to board the strange ship and we are inquiring as to his present whereabouts.

Apparently this mysterious craft did not stay long in the Mushville vicinity, as no other citizens have reported seeing the alien or his spacecraft.

****

At our next meeting, all the future writers were blabbing about what a good alien joke we pulled.

Did you know you could rent a Bigfoot costume? Not in Mushville, of course. Greta's brother Fedex'd it to us from a big city which shall remain unnamed.

A few days later I reported my scoop to the Chief.

Klaxon readers were treated to the following news:

BIGFOOT MYSTERY SOLVED BY LOCAL MEN!

Just returned from the Pacific Northwest, a local man (who wishes to remain anonymous) has some astonishing news: He claims to have the answers to many questions regarding the large hairy creatures who have remained so elusive for many decades.

"I didn't pussyfoot around," said the man, whom we'll call Mr. X. "I traveled to town Y, state Z, where Bigfeet had been glimpsed in the deep woods."

Our veteran reporter asked if he didn't mean Bigfoots for the plural, since Bigfeet would be a change in the actual name of the creature. Mr. X replied he thought Bigfeet was correct and did we want to hear the story or not. Mr. X continued, "See, I set a rope snare to catch any Bigfeet [sic] that might be about."

"Me and my buddy (whom we'll call Mr. W) hiked in to a remote spot near a creek known as (creek C). I said to (Mr. W), 'Let's use cheeseburgers for bait.', but he thought carrots would be better."

"Well, that took the cake! I said, 'They ain't rabbits! They ain't goats!'

"We set up the table with a big plate of cheeseburgers. Touch that plate and the snare would be triggered and catch your leg in the rope loop.

"We hid out of sight and waited and waited. Suddenly, a booming voice came from behind, with a Brooklyn accent: 'Hey, Bozos, here I am! I been watching you set up that snare, think I'd fall for that? Hah!' "

Mr. X and Mr. W were surprised and scared. Mr. X further related: "A hefty, hairy creature stood there, a dead ringer for any Bigfoot you ever saw. He had a .38 snubnose in a shoulder holster."

"He walked over and helped himself to the burgers, avoiding

48

the snare. He asked for ketchup, but we didn't have any."

Thinking quickly, Mr. X snapped a photograph (seen below). Even though somewhat blurred by camera motion, it clearly shows a hairy creature reaching for a plate of burgers. Also notice he was packing, as Mr. X told us.

We so far do not know the name of the personage formerly known as Bigfoot, so we will call him Mr. B.

Mr. X and Mr. W listened to an amazing tale related by the hairy being: It turns out years ago, a bunch of prisoners at a certain prison unnamed by Mr. B (call it S. Q.) volunteered to test a baldness cure in exchange for reduced time on their 100 year sentences.

It worked too well, they got hairy all over and their muscles bulged, too. They bided time and all got together and pried the steel bars like Superman would and headed for the deep forest. The whole thing was so embarrassing, the Feds didn't want to catch them, so they have been left to shift for themselves all these years. Naturally, besides being embarrassed by their appearance, they kept away from people, not wishing to be sent back to the slammer.

Mr. X reports that Mr. B was polite and thanked them for the burgers as he left, and asked that they bring ketchup next time.

The Klaxon's investigative reporting team is vigorously pursuing this unfolding story. Prison officials from possible prisons have all denied having turned any inmates into hairy Bigfoots.

****

A few nights later I related the dumpster raccoon story to a fellow at the library writer's group I just joined. Herb White's his name; wants to be a poet, "Don't mind me, but, you see, I try to rhyme, all the time."

I said, "I thought you'd like that story. You know they do throw away the leftover doughnuts, the raccoons know it. Let's mosey over there and see!"

Herb said, "Discarded pastry, could still be tasty."

Midnight. We crept toward the dark hulk of the dumpster behind the coffee shop. Suddenly yellow light streaked from an opened door; we melted into the shadows. A young lady stepped quickly to the dumpster and tossed in a big poly bag of the day's unsold doughnuts.

When she left, we grabbed them and walked into the darkness for a quick getaway. Herb led the way, four blocks to St. Jerome's Cemetery.

He had fixed a little tent shelter behind one of the big tombs and was camping there.

"What's the deal? Why come to this creepy place?" I asked.

"Not so creepy, it's where I sleepy," said Rhyming Herb.

We were about to open our goody bag when headlights came on, pointed right at us.

"Police! Don't move, guys."

It was Spence.

"Hey Spence, it's me, Ringley."

"Oh my Gawd, can't you stay outta trouble, Ringy?"

"I hope you didn't take out that hair-trigger gun of yours, Spence!"

Didn't answer, just said, "That reminds me, this would be a good place for target practice. We're past the edge of town."

"Can't camp here, y'know, my friend," he says, looking at Herb.

Herb said, "But there's room to spare; the dead don't care."

"What kind of doughnuts do you like Spence?" I asked as I opened the huge bag.

"Oh, got any Boston Creams in there?"

"Do you know this hick town has got no shooting range for the force? How the Heck can we practice? Those cans empty, there?"

Spence set up six pop cans on top of one of the tombstones about fifty feet away.

"BLAM! BLAM!" Two cans down.

"Most cops never practice the draw. Important to draw fast sometimes."

He holstered the gun. Then suddenly grabbed it and, "BLAM!" That was the shot. "WHIRRRAANNNG!" That was the ricochet. Hit the thin tombstone with that one. Smack in the middle. "CLONK!" That was a big piece falling. Right on the vase with the fresh flowers.

"&^%$#$, shot too soon, that hair trigger again!"

They probably wondered at the CVS store why Spence bought eight tubes of Superglue. He came back with it and Herb and I helped put Humpty back together again.

Herb said, "Good as new, with Superglue!"

"Hey, Rhymin' Simon, who asked you?" asked Officer Spence.

And with that he was off into the night.

****

The following week, at the next writer's meeting, I said, "We can talk about stories, or think of a hoax that nobody would believe and try to get it in the Klaxon, which is it?"

"Hoax!" "Hoax!" "Hoax!"

"Listen, I've got an idea for an interview with another anonymous person. This time Herb, since you're a stringer for the Klaxon, how about you interviewing our amazing person who can't be named?"

Herb said, "Sure thingy, Ringy."

"Anybody know who has a ham radio setup?"

Bonnie's cousin had one.

"Bonnie, think your cousin would mind putting a paper bag over his head and getting his picture taken in front of his radio set?"

"He thinks I'm crazy already, he expects such things!"

A few days later, The Daily Klaxon had more front page news:

RADIO LINK TO SPIRIT WORLD!

We present an exclusive interview with a local man who talks at will to deceased persons from far and wide who exist in what apparently is a vast spirit world. We will respect his wishes and refer to him only as Mr. X, (not to be confused with Mr. X from last week, who is a different person).

Mr. X has invented a new type of shortwave radio which he demonstrated for our reporter.

Mr. X said, "I'm a radio engineer, also I knew about theories of the so-called spirit world where we all go after death. Radio waves are invisible and penetrate invisible space, maybe that includes the spirit space invisible to us. I reasoned that we had to wait until radio engineers died and constructed radios before we could communicate."

Mr. X sent letters to hundreds of radio engineers telling them if they did land on the "other side" to be sure to construct radio sets tuned to his specifications.

Mr. X continued, "I've searched since 1978, and finally a Mr.

53

Izzy Fields, a former GE guy, sent me a signal!"

The photograph below shows Mr. X, with a paper bag over his head, in front of his special radio invention. We apologize for the blurring due to camera motion.

What follows is a verbatim transcript taken by our reporter:

Mr. X: "I'll turn it on and show you how it works."

Radio: "BLXXXP Hmmmmmmmm"

Mr. X: "Breaker, breaker, come in, Izzy."

Radio: "Hmmmmmmmm"

Mr. X: "Breaker, breaker, come in, Izzy."

Radio: "Hmmmmmmmm"

Mr. X: "He isn't always available."

Mr. X: "Izzy, Izzy, Come in, Good Buddy!"

Radio: "SLXXK! BZZZ! Oh, (Mr. X), is that you?"

Mr. X: "Yes, it's me, (Mr. X), who'd you expect, I'm the one who built the &^^%$ radio!"

Radio: "Yeah, OK, don't get touchy, maybe I'd like to talk to somebody else once in a while. Are you keeping this thing a secret?"

Mr. X: "Did you find D.B. Cooper yet? I want to ask him if he hid the money, would he mind telling me where it is?"

Radio: "Yeah, well, you know it's a big place over here. I'll telegraph the Oregon trading post."

Mr. X: "Trading post?"

Radio: "Yeah, well, like they say you can't take it with you. You got to start from scratch over here if you want anything. Everything is Do-It-Yourself projects, but there's no Home Depot. You wouldn't believe what I made this radio out of. It's a crystal set, does that tell you anything?"

Mr. X: "Izzy, what do you guys do for recreation?"

Radio: "I'm learning to haunt. If I just concentrate like meditation I can visit your side in a wispy black-and-white form, sometimes even write very faint scary letters."

Mr. X: "Can you talk louder? You're fading out."

Radio: "Yeah, I feel faded out. OK, over and out, Good Buddy. By the way, I'm not a vengeful person, but tell that &^^%%$ who dropped the safe on me I'm planning to haunt him and scare the wits out of him."

****

Next meeting we read stories. Mickey's story went like this:

A dapper man with gray hair and a neat goatee sat near me at the coffee shop. A philosophy professor?

He was talkative, in a casual way: "Busy this morning here, I

55

see. People following a behavioral pattern or habit. Come often enough to buy a coffee, in fact 21 times in a row, and you will do it forever, subject to external events, of course.

"Sir, when you are finished with your newspaper, would you mind giving it to me? I try to conserve what little money I have."

I handed over the paper. I had read enough of it, anyway.

He gave me a closer look with his owl's stare, and said, "Excuse me, but you look so familiar, did you perhaps teach at Harvard some years ago while I also taught there?"

I said, "No, sorry, you must be mistaken."

He apologized and looked over the paper.

I said to him, "I'm going to get a coffee, may I buy you one?"

He accepted and thanked me.

The old man had more to say: "This article reminds me of my student days. I studied the methods of B.F. Skinner and I learned his techniques very well."

*"Dr. Skinner demonstrated how to train chickens to turn in circles, by carefully planned rewards and so on. I found these methods had vast commercial possibilities, in fact **I accumulated millions.** Of course, I don't have that now, as I have a very bad habit. I must have gambled 21 times in a row, my friend."*

Then he leaned close and confided in a low voice, "You have been very kind to me, a stranger, after all. If you want I'll tell you how I made a large fortune. But if I do you must promise to keep it to yourself, OK?"

That was the beginning of Mickey's story. You'll have to wait until he publishes it to see how it turns out. I respect my fellow writers.

I changed my mind. Quick summary follows:

Think it was about a scam? You're right. The "professor" supposedly trains gophers to find gold by tasting sand and dirt; where there is gold dust, upstream there must be gold nuggets and veins that the dust came from. To pay gambling debts, he must sell his special gophers at ridiculously low prices, when you consider each one will find gold for you and all you have to do is feed it carrots. He has a little bag of brass filings he shows, only a quick peek, though.

Mickey got many compliments on his story.

As a joke I came to the next meeting with a gopher in a cage. Didn't say anything. Just brought it along. The writers were amused, but a library person frowned and complained. Apparently gophers are not welcome at the Mushville Public Library. Well, they don't pay any taxes, I guess.

I carried Goldie to work at the newspaper because I needed to feed and water her and she made a cute pet and besides Bonnie who is cute herself likes Goldie and thought I should keep her and not just let her go just yet.

Trouble was, Mickey showed his story to a few friends, and I suspect that is why rumors popped up that fortunes could be made if you had a smart gopher. Wouldn't that explain why this young fellow had a gopher in a cage?

Don from the used car place stopped me on the street on my way home. "Is it true that gopher there can find gold?"

"No, of course not, that was just a story that must have started a rumor."

"Look, I know, you probably want to keep it quiet. No problem, I'll keep quiet. How about just telling me who you got it from, $20 bucks if you tell me, why not?"

"Don, I trapped this gopher yesterday, it can't find gold."

"Why would you trap a stupid gopher, everybody else hates 'em and tries to get rid of 'em! $50 bucks, just the name of the person who trains 'em."

"There is no person, Don."

"You mean he's dead? This is the last trained gopher, that's why you're guarding him so well?"

Just then Spence pulls up in Cruiser No. 4.

"Hey, Ringy, bad news, I got to ticket you for illegal trapping, $500. Stiff ain't it?"

"WHAAT??, Spence…."

"Think Herb's done work? I have to find him. You come too, I need your help."

I got in, with Goldie in her cage, and we sped off to the cemetery. Herb is there, but he's flustered. Fired from his bakery job (baked 50 adobe bricks instead of bread), now all his stuff is gone.

"A double whammy," said Herb, "even my jammies!"

Spence explained to Herb, "Hey, Buddy, the Chief found out you were here and nailed you on vagrancy, sent Norris to grab all your stuff, sorry, you know, I told you you can't camp here.

"But you can get it back, in fact, the inventory is right here. Norris said that's a cute teddy bear you got. He says thanks for the 'Girls of Vegas' mags.

"Right now you both can help me. There's this boat adrift in the river, the Chief told me to take the Police Launch and retrieve it, gotta hurry, current's carrying it away, y'know."

Siren again, ducks and chicks and geese scurried, we made the riverfront in about a minute, Spence tellin' what happened yesterday.

"You think you guys got trouble. Hey, Lordy, Lordy. The department has three motorcycles and Kresge challenged me to a race, $20 bucks bet on it, how could I turn that down? Two things went wrong. First, The Farmer in the Dell reported us because we went across a little bit of his cornfield.

"Second, when we got to where the trail crosses that sandbar on Zip's Creek, I bogged and dumped, big dents in the Chief's bike! Kresge had a fit laughing and I'm still mad at him. Naturally, we ain't supposed to race police bikes, so the Chief is writing up some awful report on us."

At the shore we could see the expensive thirty-footer with nobody aboard, just drifting. We all clambered aboard the patrol boat. Looked like a lobster boat which was old and decrepit. Spence fired it up and it churned water as we turned out from shore. Engine made a racket but we moved along smartly.

I stepped on something that moved, and looked down. It was a six-foot black snake! Herb said, "There's a snake, that's no mistake!"

Spence said, "I hate snakes, get an ax!" No ax in sight, snake is dodging around trying to get away.

Spence says, "Stand back!" as he lines up a shot.

"Don't shoot a hole in the boat!"

"BLAM!" A complete miss. You could see the bullet hole. "BLAM!" Snake is moving faster, no fool. "BLAM!" Got 'em. Snake, you messed with the wrong deputy this time.

"Spence, should we head for shore? We got three holes."

"Naw, plenty of time, only little holes."

The drifter was still way downstream. It seemed to be in the faster current.

I lifted a deck panel. We had about a foot of water. We were lower in the water and going slower. Water soon got up over our ankles.

"I got an idea, find some lifejackets!" says Spence. We did. Luckily we had left Goldie on shore, 'cause we didn't have any gopher-size lifejackets.

Water was getting up to our knees. Captain Spence said, "We'd better head for shore."

He cut the wheel toward the opposite shore since it was closer. The boat turned as fast as a Galapagos Turtle. We were about 100 feet from shore when the engine started sucking water and stopped with a thud.

Our lifejackets made for an easy swim to shore. We dragged up on a dock, nobody around. We looked back across the water. No Mushville police patrol boat. In the gathering dusk we could barely see the thirty-footer, just a speck it was so far downstream.

Nobody said a word. We all walked four blocks toward the center of Chugtown until we got to the tracks. A forty-car train was clanking and starting to move. One at a time we easily swung aboard an open boxcar.

If the train kept going, by morning we would be 400 miles from Mushville annoyances.

I started to sing a little tune from long ago. I happened to know the words. You know that song "The Three Caballeros"?

I sang the first line.

Spence said, "Ringy, you are a crazy guy."

Herb agreed, but after I sang a few more lines, they started to join in and we got louder. We faked most of the lines, but didn't sound bad for drowned rats.

As we sang we passed slowly by some people waiting for a passenger train. Can you believe it? That stone-faced crowd applauded as we passed by.

Somebody called, "How about 'On the Road Again'?"

Hey, Spence knew that one. Take it, Spence!

Can You Hear Me Now, Scar?

"Scar! Get this crate higher, they're shootin' at us!"

The twin engines' throaty rumble rose into a higher register and we skimmed past the airport hanger roof.

I clung to the wheel strut, dangling, my face against the fat rubber tire. A few feet above me the rotund one named "Scar" sat in the pilot's seat. His two companions had thrown me bodily from the hijacked plane, but I managed to catch onto the landing gear.

"Scar? May I speak with you?" I called.

"Shut up, you &^%$%^&!" he barked.

"Apparently you are being pursued by the police, is that a fair assumption, Scar? I heard those sirens."

Since I was contemplating entering the Theological Seminary

of DELETED in the fall, I had been thinking a lot about how important it is in life to make the right choices, and to help others choose the righteous path in this world.

"Scar, may I interrupt you for a moment?

"Let me ask you a point blank question, Scar. Which would you say is more important, the spiritual life or the material life? Think before you answer, please."

"BANG! BANG!" Two shots, apparently directed toward me, missed.

"Scar, was that you shooting? We won't make progress this way, I can assure you. I don't mean to be brusque with you, but, now, how old are you? You are not a young man, and you would be wise to consider where you are headed with this behavior."

"BANG! BANG!"

"You there, shooting. What's your name? They called you 'Butch', didn't they? Butch, stop shooting at me, I want to talk to you, too. It's important…it's not about me, it's about you!"

Someone called, "Shake him off, Scar, I can't get a bead on him!"

The plane tipped wildly and lurched….we went into a sickening skid sideways.

Suddenly an object struck me on the head and landed on the plane structure; the shooter had dropped his weapon, I could see it right by my nose as I gripped the plane's wheel strut.

A police helicopter came from below; they had a bullhorn and someone called out: "LAND OR WE SHOOT YOU DOWN!"

The hijackers answered with a burst of machine gun fire, "RAT-TAT-TAT-TAT-TAT!"....directed toward the police helicopter.

Then I heard the "CRACK , CRACK,..... CRACK,..." of repeated high-powered rifle fire...I could see little flame spurts at the muzzles as they shot at our plane.

The bullhorn voice from the helicopter called out, "STOP, CAPTAIN, THAT'S THE MAYOR'S SON, PETE ROGERS! HE'S HOLDING ONTO THE LANDING GEAR! DON'T SHOOT!"

I corrected him, however, "NO, I JUST LOOK LIKE HIM, I'M HAROLD CARMEN. IT'S A COMMON MISTAKE. IT'S FUNNY, EVEN THE MAYOR CALLED ME 'PETE' ONCE...WE WERE ALL AT THE BEACH..."

"CRACK , CRACK,..... CRACK,..." The rifle fire started again, but did not seem to hit anything important. The plane was faster, and we pulled some distance ahead of our pursuers, careening erratically.

The criminals had apparently been distracted from shooting at me.

"Scar, Are you listening to me? It is your future you know. You know in your heart...."

"BANG! BANG!"

You know, when a bullet comes close to you, there is a whistling sound. Ever hear a teakettle? Like that.

Now, more planes approached, Air Force jets. They buzzed us and I could see they were lining up for a broadside shot. I could see the flaming trajectory of a Tomahawk air-to-air missile headed our way.

You know, when an air-to-air missile comes close to you, there is a whistling sound. Not a teakettle, more of "WHOOO-OOSSHHH" sound. Like if you held a vacuum cleaner hose up sucking on your ear. Didn't hit us.

I had an idea. I would simply shoot some holes in the gas tank, and the Cessna would run out of gas and just coast down. I maneuvered enough to hold on with my arms and grip the .45 automatic and then let rip with a few shots into the belly of the plane, and sure enough, fuel gushed out into the air stream.

However, my happiness was short-lived, as the fuel caught fire. You know, it is an interesting effect, the way the high speed air stream interacts with the gasoline, it's the same as a blowtorch, used by plumbers in the old days; they used gasoline, too,... wait, some used kerosene.

"Scar, I've shot holes in the gas supply, we're coming down, and I'd advise you to just give up to the authorities."

No answer,... Hah!, maybe Scar is doing some thinking. We glided lower and lower and as luck would have it, coasted into a farmyard and as we neared a haystack I let go and landed in the hay.

The plane skidded to a halt in a muddy farm pond, and the water extinguished the flames. I had suffered broken ribs, but rushed over to the plane.

Although both wounded in the body and legs, Butch and his companion had exited already, and I helped the also bloodied Scar get out of the cockpit. My shooting and police rifle fire had effected a few wounds, but no deaths, so we all thanked the Almighty for that. At least I did. The police helicopter arrived and they soon handcuffed the three.

At the hospital they taped up my broken ribs and soon I was rolled into one of the rooms. What a surprise, there was a police guard there and in the bed next to mine, who else but ...Scar! The very same Scar of my recent acquaintance.

"Scar! I trust you are recovering OK? It's me again. You were shooting at me, remember?"

My only answer was a kind of moan..."Ooooooh.... Oooohhh Aaagggghhhhhh...."

"Perhaps now you will have time to reflect on your wounds and burns. You might wonder as I do.... that perhaps the Good Lord is trying to tell you something?"

A prune-faced woman stood nearby. I remarked pleasantly, "Oh, this little package of mashed vegetables is delicious, Nurse Grimley! There is just one thing you forgot."

I pointed to my lips and smiled broadly, though the stitches pulled a little. "I was trying to remember that song in the musical 'Annie!' It's about smiling... Oh, I remember, 'You're Never Fully Dressed Without a Smile'. Oh, that's so truc, don't you think, Nurse?

"Scar, I see from your hospital record sheet that you're from the Bronx. My brother, you know, used to travel right near there on his way to Yale. Small world, isn't it?

"Scar, I'm still waiting for your answer you know, the question about Grace and Redemption?"

"Oooohhh Aaagggghhhhhh...."

"Scar, Let me relate a short tale that pertains to our conversation... It's called 'The Bad Squirrel' and I... it's really funny, I know this story so well, because I memorized it for Sunday School when I was 4 years old! Ha! I remember I didn't get it quite right, though, Sister Bernadette, the dear, pointed it out at the debriefing... I said the squirrel was from North Dakota, but it was actually South Dakota!

"But, let me continue....."

"Oooohhh Aaagggghhhhhh...."

The Call of Duty

You can put this book up against your top books: *Sergeant DELETED and the Missing Gold.* I was hoping to get into the Mounties after reading it. They always get their man, you know. I read it in the above book, which I can recommend.

I lost my good garage job when I dropped the engine through the Jag chassis. Then that TV rerun came on about *Sergeant DELETED and the Horseshoe Thieves*, where they crush his hat so he smacks the villain a good one for that insult! Don't mess with Mounties, you dirt bag! I was being called by Providence, and I traveled to the Mountie Headquarters to apply.

Lt. McGregor, the Mountie recruiter, was real nice and said yes they could use some more people, there weren't no crowd waiting to serve since Canada is a godforsaken icebox of a country to be patrolling, especially on a horse. I don't remember his exact words. He showed me his hat and I even tried it on briefly. In the office there they had a big fire going in the stone fireplace, with some fatback pork sizzlin' away, Boy, it smelled good!

They gave me a physical exam, and he asked, "What is this black walnut-sized object in your head that shows up in the x-ray picture?" I explained that I was a professional boxer briefly and that black thing is a little battery-powered electronic device that reduces your reflex time, called the Speed-Punch. They plugged the hole with a little bottle cap after they put it in. Doesn't hurt, but I sometimes dream that I have a walnut in my head.

I had to admit that the Speed-Punch didn't do much for my career...I was faster, but still Blacky Luccio knocked me flat...that was my last fight. Speed-Punch is not approved by any of the boxing commissions, anyway. Plus the electronic activity has some side effects: If I smell flowers, I get all jumpy, I hop like a rabbit instead of walking, and if I tried to light a cigarette, I'd burn your nose. That's only around flowers or perfume that's strong enough. I can hear voices at a distance, whether they're there or not. Also, I keep wanting to eat popcorn all the time.

In the x-rays they noticed the two bullets in my thigh and side, too. That was an embarrassing thing. Me and Gabe were fooling around drawing on each other with six-shooters and he plugged me a couple. He apologized for the mistake.

The recruiter also asked, "Why did you bring your ventriloquist's dummy to the interview?", referring to Kenny in my lap. I explained that, of course, Kenny looked like just a wooden dummy, but he was a real live friend of mine, just small, so I carried him a lot, he's only got little legs. We wanted to be a team in the Mounties.

He was nice to Kenny, too, even though Kenny made a few jokes about Mounties ironing their hats and like that. "You got a Black and Decker Polisher for those brass buttons?" he asked. Kenny's like that.

Unfortunately, I only got 30 percent on the written exam, not 80 percent or higher. They were nice but it wasn't long before I was out on the porch, my Mountie career ended before it started. I sat on the porch steps. I didn't cry, but Kenny got a little teary-eyed. I sat and thought and kicked the dirt idly with my foot. Kenny kicked, too, but unfortunately couldn't reach it with his baby-sized legs.

Later that day I was hitchhiking on that same back road in Saskatchewan when instead of a car, some horseback riders were trotting along and presently stopped by a field loaded with a thousand steers. They didn't notice Kenny and me sitting under a willow tree. Suddenly these riders busted the fence all apart! Then they rode through and started herding all them cows out through the break in the fence!

I stepped out and hollered, "Hey! You're rustlers, ain't you?" One of 'em galloped over and swung at me with his riding crop, but I guess my Speed-Punch was still working and I grabbed it in mid-air and yanked the fellow off his horse, and he fell in a heap. The other gang members weren't near and paid no attention in the commotion of dust and noise of all those cattle.

They were gonna steal 'em all and head for open country, parts unknown. Being an expert rider, it took me no time to borrow the varmint's horse, a strong bay stallion. Kenny said, "Wait, get his gun too, we might need it." So I relieved the dazed outlaw of his six-gun, holster, belt, and bullets.

With my long-distance hearing, I heard the leader call the plan: "Take 'em up Indian Road to the secret corral!"

I now cut across some fields, jumping fences where required and was soon far ahead and I came to the sign for Indian Road. "Hah!" says I, as I quickly removed the sign with my Leatherman pliers tool, carefully saving the screws and nuts. On I rode; the horse was sweaty, I was sweaty, Kenny was sweaty, too, and took out a tiny handkerchief to wipe his brow.

Further down this dusty road I came to a sign: "Mountie Headquarters" and a road leading into the big compound. Dismounting, I quickly put the "Indian Road" sign in place of the "Mountie" sign.

Then Kenny and I proceeded into the main office. "Rustlers on their way! They'll be here soon!" I warned.

The recruiter, Lt. McGregor, recognized me. But instead of a big "Hello", he whispered to the person at the desk. With my enhanced hearing, I heard: "It's that crazy guy again! Call the Sergeant-at-Arms, he's got a gun this time!"

I calmly explained that about five gunmen would be arriving along with a thousand big Herefords, but they weren't getting ready for that. Instead, several Mounties came in the front door with their revolvers drawn and backed me and Kenny against the wall. "Don't move, and hand over the gun, Sir!" Not waiting for an answer he whipped out handcuffs, however, my fast reflexes anticipated his move and I grabbed the cuffs out of his hand.

Then Kenny, who was no dummy, grabbed some of the bullets from my pocket and threw them into the fire!

Some of the Mounties rushed towards the fire, some of the Mounties ran back from the fire. Maybe it's not covered in Mountie School what to do.

"BANG! BANG! PING!" The exploding bullets were enough diversion to allow Kenny and me to dash out the side door.

Outside, the huge fenced compound was being flooded with the stolen herd, hooves thundering, with the mounted drivers yelling behind them. We now remounted the bay and I spurred the horse toward the front gate. With dust clouds all around the scurvy villains didn't realize they had delivered the beeves to the wrong address.

Soon the red-coated Mounties came running, well-armed and inquiring the meaning of this unexpected cattle delivery, (Hadn't I just got through telling them, they're rustlers, remember?). Not wishing to talk with the Mounties, the horsemen retreated, thinking to escape, but I had closed the gate behind them and even used the handcuffs I still had with me to secure it.

Those guys were mad! They were all wisely surrendering, but one snarling guy apparently blamed me for his troubles, as though it was my fault he had chosen a crime career, and fired shots directly at me. Then he was out of ammo and dejectedly gave up. I was relieved to find I was not hit, but…poor Kenny! He's been hit! There was a round hole through his little chest! A big hole, I could put my finger right through it!

Back inside, I called for a first aid kit and the Mountie medic helped me bandage Kenny's gaping wound and make him comfortable on a little doll bed they happened to have. The medic took me aside. "He may not make it, Sir..."

"You don't know Kenny, he's sturdy as an oak...in fact, he's made of oak," I replied.

I modestly explained that I was the hero who discovered the cattle theft and redirected the gang to Mountie Headquarters and trapped them by closing the gate. They were amazed and pleased. It was a feather in their Smokey Bear hats to capture that gang.

Some aspirin and a shot of Canadian Whiskey, and some Bondo Body Filler brought Kenny around to feeling better. It was late in the day by then, and they paid for me and Kenny to stay at a local cabin court. We headed over there. Hey, there's TV! I found a place to buy some popcorn and we watched some movies and hit the hay.

Next day, a funny thing happened. Seems the Mounties were going to get medals out of the gang capture, and they requested the governor to grant a special waiver of the rules...so they offered me The Full Mountie, (that's a commission with first pair of boots free), plus the same for Kenny, with a complete little Mountie uniform just his size! I was flabbergasted!

'Course, I had to tell them that Kenny and I had decided to join a circus instead, after seeing that terrific movie, "The Greatest Show on Earth!"

Author's Night

Dale: "Tonight on The Dale Midland Show we have not one but two of America's most distinguished authors, Mark Grebin and Joe Doaks."

Joe: "Thanks, Dale, I appreciate it and I want to say to everyone how much I admire the genius of Mark Grebin's work."

Mark: "Ha, ha. I think if there is any literary genius here tonight, it belongs to this man, Joe Doaks! I loved your novel Blabbynab the Clown and the Lollipop Thieves. I have only one tiny quibble with it...you sometimes use the recessive pluperfect voice a little too freely...it's a small thing, I know..."

Joe: "I always welcome critiques, especially from a literary giant, such as you. When time permits perhaps we can review the particular place...."

Mark: "It's where the captain of the Titanic tells Blabbynab: 'No, you can't take your clown bicycle into the lifeboat.', and Blabbynab squirts tears from his eyes..."

Joe: "Perhaps you didn't realize that I was just using some sufficiated irony there...."

Dale: "Wait, wait...for me and others... what's sufficiated irony, Joe?"

Joe: "It's a bit subtle,...it's like throwing open the sash and there's Santa, but only seven reindeer! So you say, "Gosh, is one of them sick?" When you write to Santa you have to say you hope everything is OK with the missing reindeer. This could go on year after year! "

Dale: "Joe, some critics think that the main character in your most recent novel has a resemblance to Mark Grebin; I'm referring to your novel Mark Grebin: The Decline and Fall of a Hack Writer.

Joe: "Oh, ha, ha, ha,... no, of course not, the poor demented slob in my novel is not modeled on my friend Mark Grebin, it's just one of those coincidences. The career paths do match, I have to admit."

Mark: "Joe, my friend, forgive me for saying so, but I do think that is suspiciously like the kind of tasteless, even blasphe-mous, humor you sometimes indulge in..."

Joe: "Blasphemous, ha, ha, you must be joking....! Like what?"

Mark: "How about your story in the *Utica Pallbearer's*

Journal? Gwendolyn has a pet turtle named Theresa! Are you saying Mother Theresa looks like a turtle?"

Joe: "No, but I may write a story with a dodo named Mark Grebin!"

Mark: "Joe, speaking of dodos, I have to admire your use of the 'Dumb Author' technique, where you use big words, but misuse them!"

Joe: "Hmmm, I don't remember misusing any big words...."

Mark: "For example, in your story, 'Alcoholic Chipmunk', when you said the refulmencious quality of indulgence..."

Joe: "I don't quite follow your jaxtinity, here, Mark, do you mean holmonbanity would have been a better word?"

Dale: "You're both way ahead of me...what's holmonbanity ?"

Mark: "Holmonbanity is when the person in front of you in a cafeteria line takes the last chocolate cupcake, so you pretend to stumble, knocking his tray over and stepping on the cupcake. You have a little remorse, but it fades quickly and you are glad you did it."

Joe: "Of course, you would know better than me, but I'd say holmonbanity means, say, you're a pilot coming in for a landing, two feet above the runway, and a flight attendant shouts, 'YOU FORGOT TO LOWER THE LANDING GEAR! WE'RE GOING TO DIE!' so you say, 'Here, you fly the &^%$%^ plane , Smartypants!'."

Mark: "Forgive me, I forgot you have won the Pulitzer Prize so undoubtedly you know better than I! I have only won The Pushkin, The Kazakhstan National Medal, and …."

Joe: "I'm not surprised you won the Pushkin, you have all those rash youthful experiences to draw upon…"

Mark: "Ha, ha, what youthful experiences….?"

Joe: "Well, in your autobiography you mention the armed robberies, …"

Mark: "No, no, I mentioned when I was a kid, I snitched a candy bar."

Joe: "And that incident where you opened the emergency exit on the school bus, kids went out the back, resulting in seven deaths."

Mark: "Wait… The bus was stopped, the deaths were Danny's crickets that got squashed! Perhaps, Joe, you have won no Pushkin because of certain plagiaristic tendencies!"

Joe: "And, specifically, Dear Friend…???"

Mark: "The family had a dog named 'Spot' in my *Clam Digger's Journal* story…but then in *The West Ohio Harvester* your story has the line: ' "See Spot run!" said Sally.'."

Joe: "Ha, ha, ha, but Dear Friend, your 'Spot' could have been a cat, you carelessly don't specify… or a raccoon, or even a weasel, like his author!"

Dale: "Gentlemen, gentlemen, let's not be too excitable,

please....

"Tell me what other experiences have led to your maturity as writers, ...anyone?"

Mark: "Well, I'm sure Joe can draw on his experience of seven Drunk and Disorderly arrests..."

Joe: "That was only six Drunk and Disorderly arrests.... Mark, maybe you can draw on your experience of evading combat in World War II by pretending you had amnesia and couldn't remember your name (until your miraculous recovery in 1945)."

Mark: "Joe, I'm sure that we all have to thank you for spending your war years in the military writing 'Sergeant Chipmunk's Grammar and Punctuation Tips'!"

Mark: "Dale, if I may see that story collection, the book Joe gave you, ...I'll just... RRRRRIP!   remove the mention of 'Spot'.....at least this copy won't have plagiarized material in it!!"

Joe: "Have you had lunch, Mark? Maybe you'd like to eat those pages! If you can chew them with those yellow false teeth of yours!"

Mark: "Speaking of false, where'd you get your toupee? ......Sears and Roebuck?"

Joe: "Yes, that is a policeman you see approaching, Mark, I called on my cell phone a minute ago while you were babbling... he'll be interested in your theft of the candy bars, which I happen to know is not beyond the statute of limitations for West Virginia…."

Mark: "Put up your dukes, Doaks!"

Joe: "Hah! Dukes? Those are baby fists you've got!"

"THUMP! BAM!"

Mark: "Take that! (a famous boxer) taught me that punch!"

"WHAP!"

Joe: "(another famous boxer) taught me that one!"

Mark: "Here's one for Mother Theresa! BAM!"

Joe: "Let go of me, Mark! Officer, did you bring your cuffs?"

Dale: "That's all we have time for, Folks. We have so much to cover, Part II is scheduled for next week, be sure to tune in."

"BAM! THUMP! CRASH! POW!"

America's Dumbest Garage Mechanic

"Heh, heh, heh."

I was on my back under Mossey's old Toyota, beatin' on the @%^$## muffler hangers. Between hammering I heard the boss in the office trying not to be heard... but he was chucklin' away. Usually he's a grouch.

"Hey, what's funny in there, Boss?" I scooted out on my creeper. He was looking at some video from our security cameras, and he turned it off quick.

"Nothin'."

He paused.

"Oh Heck, I might as well tell you, Wes, they'll be sure to call you! Heh, heh."

Well, yeah, he told me, and I was cussin' mad, the double-crossin' coot! Hard to believe, here it is, you tell me, wouldn't you be mad?

Seems there's this low-life TV show producer in New York City. He's putting on a show....it's called "America's Dumbest Garage Mechanic". Real stupid idea for a show. This twerp producer's got money from robbin' people or somethin' so he went around to garages all over and put secret cameras to spy on mechanics, to see if anybody would do something that made them look dumb. Must be illegal, but there it is, he's doin' it.

Cuss me all foot-stomp! It makes me mad! Gimpy, the skunk, got paid and put in cameras here, right here like they're the FBI or somebody. I wondered why he put in all those security cameras in this dinky garage!

I yelled at Gimpy, told him I was quitting and so there with your spy cameras!

'Course next day I came back, 'cause I just started this job and I need the money, who don't need some money, right?

A week went by. Tell you the truth I forgot all about it till the phone rang and it was...guess who? Mr. Spy-Producer from New York!

I was holding an ice cube against my nose, reason was the serpentine belt on the Dodge came flyin' up and whacked my nose a good one. It was adjusted perfect when I put it in, I don't know what happened, must is it was defective from the get-go. That's why they call them serpentine, trust 'em like you would a rattlesnake!

I couldn't hear so good because of the nose problem, but the fool was talking up a storm. Wanted me to come to his studio, I was selected special from thousands to be on his stupid quiz program, could be to win money. Well, no, I preferred to stay here and work at my miserable mechanic's helper job and not go to be laughed at by idiots that might watch his illegal TV show that would soon be shut down by the FDIC or somebody. "SLAM!" That was me putting back the phone.

However, that wasn't the end of it, they called again and talked to Gimpy and Gimpy worked on me with smooth talk. Said he was sorry, blah, blah, and it would be great for business if I was to appear on a big show and all. It was all just some fun, you know. The big thing is, he said it was sure I'd get some money, even if you didn't win any big prize, even the contestants that didn't win would get at least a quick $1,000 and they paid your transportation, room and eats, good hotel, not a sleazebag joint, you know.

Well, I pouted, and said, "No way, Hose-A." Next day, though, some promo stuff came in the mail. Photos of the show rehearsals already going on.

Gimpy calls out: "Whooooee! Look at these four knock-me-down extremely fine girls....the host's helpers!"

"Forget it," I says, "I don't want to hear another word about it, forget it, I'm not going!"

The plane trip to New York was uneventful, except the little food tray had no instructions, so I balanced my free soda and food things on my knees and that didn't work so well, it spilt on my neighbor and my stewardess was a male, not my preferred gender, however, nice enough, and he explained how the little shelf worked, but it was too late to keep eating then, anyway. That's how it goes.

See, there was a problem that came up. I did get my grip, finally, had to ask some people. They've got a new thing there that brings all the bags from behind a curtain, like the baggage guys don't want anybody to see 'em, pretty funny. Everybody just stands there and after a while the bags come out like train cars but without wheels, just the flat machine carried 'em. So I got my bag. Big problem was the airport location.

See, I had thought the airport was just a walk from that New York hotel address, but it's a sight farther. I walked about three hours and didn't seem to be getting closer, and was getting tired. Fellow was sitting on some steps so I figured I would, too. He had a bottle in a paper bag. Shopped for just the one thing, I guess.

"Did you walk from the airport, too?" I asked, friendly-like.

"You got a buck?" he asks.

"Naw, hunting season ain't on yet in Punch County," I explained. I told him how I was ready this year with the .30-30 I traded and got in a deal with Ned and Buster. That was a funny one. See, Ned wanted to try arrow hunting, and I had my Elkhorn brand bow set, but you would not call it a set, I suppose, 'cause I'd lost all the arrows that came along with the bow and were the recommended type of arrow for it.

But I had just the tires that Ned needed, and Buster gave me the .30-30, a Marlin, then to pay him back Ned is gonna give

Buster the beat-up canoe that his cousin from Delmar borrowed, (Good luck with that, if you ask me, but I'll say nothing more about his cousin except I'd hate to have his liquor bill).

Fellow says, "Get lost you &%#%& Bozo!" I gathered he didn't want to talk further about hunting, and I kept on walking from there.

Ninety-Seventh Street. Ninety-Eighth Street. I got to One Hundred. I was beginning to see a pattern, even though it was dark out. There was a little fountain with some benches. I was bushed, so I stretched out to rest a bit. Cop car pulled up and he said, "Can't sleep here, Buddy." Asked me questions, kinda nosy, really. Came out that I was headed to go be on a TV show.

"What show?" he kept asking, so I had to tell him, "America's Dumbest Garage Mechanic." Turns out he knew all about the show, read it in the papers, his brother is a mechanic. "Listen, my brother is as dumb as they come! How can he get on that show?" was his question. Like I could pull strings or something, get his brother on, qualified or not.

"Hop in, Dude, I'll take you there," he says, more friendly now that he wants something. High speed trip south, used those blinking lights a few times so as not to slow down, drops me at the hotel, gives me little card from the gas station where his brother worked, wrote carefully "Milton P. Xavier", that's his brother's name, on the card. I said, yes, I'd tell them about his brother, but had to tell him don't be disappointed if his brother isn't dumb enough, they get a lot of applicants. Just didn't want to promise anything, nice guy, really.

The hotel was a relief, once I got to my room. This hotel had a U-Drive-It elevator! Once the hotel lady explained it, I could run it fine, except I didn't try the equals sign and some others. I liked going down the best. Floor 20 clear down to Floor B, that was the best. I was on my third trip and it stopped at Floor 7, young lady got on, I said, "Do you want me to drive?" She got off again, must have forgot something.

Got to my room. I looked around for a hidden camera pointed at me. Since I was recently spied upon, I don't think I was being paranormal there, do you?

Nice soft bed. There was a little thing wrapped up on the pillow, well, I called down to the main desk, "Is it soap, maybe or what?" She said, "It's to eat, a fancy mint." That's what you get at a New York hotel, I guess. I ate that, nice mint flavor. The flat ones in the bathroom weren't so good, not sweet at all. New York for ya!

I forgot to tell you, when I first got there I saw these newspaper boxes, put-your-money-in boxes near the hotel. I could see through the glass the green alien story, so I put coins in, but the darned thing didn't open up! Got it after a bit, but had to turn the whole tin box upside down and use my Leatherman pliers on it, then it sprang it's little door.

Lucky I would get to New York just when the big news came out, and I could get the good reporting news about it. You've probably heard by now. I bought two copies of the Natural Enquirer newspaper (one to send home to my sister Petunia, we don't get the big city papers back to home).

I read it right away, well, except I skipped the big words, who doesn't? I asked my friend at the hotel desk, Paula, did she see the thing about the aliens right on Coney Island, which is somewhere not far but smaller than Long Island which is a big one. She was aware, but inexplicably, not worried!?

Next day, I put on my Sunday suit again and went to the studio. I ain't used to wearin' that suit and tie. I'll be honest, I ain't been to church in a long time (never).

Got to the studio. A lot of people milling around. The set has this old beat-up car with no tires, and the hood propped open.

We have to put on these mechanic's outfits, then stand behind boxes with fake tools sticking out (foam rubber). Mine is like a train engineer suit, striped, and too big. Billy got the (famous oil company) clothes and hat. I tried to trade with him but he wouldn't. They are hurrying us like crazy…studio time is so expensive, you know, get moving, we have to start!

We have to call Danny "Chief". He's got a ball cap that says "Chief Mechanic". Studio audience is big, hundreds. Don't these people have jobs? They got time to come here in the middle of the &%$@* day!

Chief explains the rules…get one wrong, they show a video of you bein' dumb! From the spy cameras. I never shoulda come here!

I'm Contestant Number One. First question: "Who started the Ford Motor Company?" I couldn't think of anybody, so the Chief shows the video …Oh heckers. It's me when I lowered the car hoist down, 3,000 pound car crushed my rolling toolbox, with all the tools spilling out all over! Then that tipped the car and rolled it right off the rack. I got out of the way quick! "Ha, ha, ha!" The crowd thought it was funny.

That was my good tools there, Folks!

Next question, got it wrong, too. Egypt ain't our driest state. Now they show me using a propane torch and the big flames coming out from under the hood and I jumped back and the tires all fell on me. "Ha, ha, ha!" Very amusing, I'm sure.

Same thing, the odometer question, not used to test for car odors like I thought, who knew? Now the video is the time I took the tool off the compressed air hose and it started whipping out of control all around the shop, OK, I did hide under the bench 'til the tank was empty. Very funny.

I'd better get some money out of this, is all I'm thinking.

Well, funny thing happened, I wasn't the only one to miss questions. Chief went through five contestants, five questions each, not a single right answer!

Good thing it was taped and not live because it was about then Mickey, the producer, comes out from the side and throws his papers on the floor.

"What the %$&*#% Danny, you stupid $%#&?% !!! We can't show this %&$*# disaster!"

Danny gets mad and throws his "Chief" hat down and stomps on it. He swears at Mickey back.

Contestant Number Three, Charley, with the "(another oil Company)" hat asks, "What about our $1,000 guaranteed, even if we didn't win?"

"No, no, if the show doesn't go on, no money, it's in your

contract," says Mickey.

Now the contestants got some riled, me too. They started throwing the foam mechanic's tools from the set at Mickey and Danny.

Crowd was booing and shouting: "Hit him, Danny!" "Hit him, Mickey!" "You chicken!"

The producer grabs Danny and wrestles him, knocking him into the jalopy car with the hood up...hood falls down on Mickey's head. "DONK!" I bet that hurt.

"OK, OK, Show's over... get outta here." Danny sends the crowd away...they're all moaning and booing. Can't blame them there, what a lousy show. Them hard questions, how could anybody answer 'em!

Everybody pretty much cleared out. I was getting ready to go, too.

Mickey was sitting on the floor, catching his breath. A lady helped him swab some of the blood from his forehead.

I squat down next to him. "Mickey, before I forget, I know a real nice fellow, who has a brother, his brother's a garage mechanic, he'd like to get on the show is what I mean, I have his card here somewhere...."

"Get outta here, you &*&%$% idiot!" was all he said. No manners at all.

Paula at the hotel helped me get back to the airport. She had a plan where I didn't have to walk for hours. First she stapled a note to my sleeve with instructions, just in case. Then she talked to a man in a car, all I had to do was pay the fee. Not cheap, but right to the airport.

I got back, and scolded Gimpy some good and plenty for getting me into such a mess.

But funny thing was, you know, I didn't expect it, but the phone rang soon after and it was the famous movie producer DELETED. Seems he was in the audience during the show and he saw the videos of the garage mishaps that happened to me. Real funny, he thought. Maybe I was a good candidate to be a dumb mechanic in a movie.

I modestly said, some of those others must be pretty dumb, none of them could answer the questions, you know. He said, that is true, but you look the dumbest, Wes. I thanked him for his confidence in me and we talked further. That was how I came to play the lead in the movie, maybe you've heard of it, "America's Dumbest Garage Mechanic". I got a fee and a percentage. Around 5 or 6 million, so far. Sequel next year.

Cat-O-Matic

My Cat-O-Matic electronic cat language translator arrived in the mail! I plugged it in and said "Testing! Testing!" into the microphone and the little speaker made a "Meoooawwoo, meoawooo" catlike sound.

Fluffy jumped up from her nap and scanned the room. She leaped on the couch back and looked behind it.

"Hello, Fluffy, it's me talking!" I said.

"*Hey, Dingbat, are you talking to me*??" she answered.

"Yes, Fluffy! Isn't it great, now we can have a little cat chat!" I said.

"*Please, Dilbert, my name isn't Fluffy. To you, it's 'Your Royal Highness Queen Cleopatra II',*" she corrected me.

"I'm excited, Fluffy, I mean Cleo, now you'll understand me

and you can come when I call you."

"Dream on, Buster Brown," said Cleo. She got comfortable to continue her nap.

"Wait, don't you want to talk any more? This is a communication breakthrough for man and the animal kingdom; you can be one of the first cats to be understood! You can tell me what it's like to be a cat."

"It's very boring," said Cleo in a bored voice.

"Do you want to know about me, your owner, where I grew up and where I went to school, and my career...?"

"No." Cleo napped on.

"Cleo, now you'll be able to make special cat food requests."

Cleo napped on.

"Cleo, I can read interesting things to you. See this magazine 'Cat Fancier'? See.... pictures of cats... ads for cat toys!"

Cleo opened one eye. *"What's a cat toy?"* she asked.

I held the magazine close to Cleo. I pointed to numerous catnip mice and little jiggly fluffy mice on strings, jingle balls, and wind-up chipmunks.

"I'd like one of those and one of those and that cat scratching post with all the cubbyholes," she allowed. *"What are those?"* she asked as she pointed with her paw at some cat books.

"Books, see, I have some around the house here, let me show you."

I read her <u>The Cat in the Hat</u>. She laughed some little cat laughs and said, *"Pretty funny, Dingleberry. Read me another one."*

I read some more. "Well, I've read five books, aren't you tired?"

"I want those cat toys!" said Queen Cleopatra II.

We went to the store to buy cat toys. After that, we went to the library to get more cat books to read. I read 20 cat books.

"Cleo, I'm tired now, don't you want to take a nap, now?"

"Let's go, Kokomo, keep reading!"

I read 20 more cat books. Cleo decided she wanted to *write* a cat story, just like the book stories. I got pencil and paper and wrote what she dictated.

"This is good, McGee, but can't you draw the pictures, too, like in <u>The Cat in the Hat</u>?"

I illustrated her cat story. (Interesting plot...a cat chased a mouse. And then chased another mouse.)

"I feel I could be a successful author. I want to write a whole series, starring my principal character, the mysterious and beautiful 'Queenie The Magnificent'," Cleo said with a burst of enthusiasm.

For some reason the Cat-O-Matic suddenly stopped working (because I pulled the plug). I said words but no cat sounds came out.

I looked at Cleo. She looked at me and said, "Meeughe meeeeoooww muge meeeeoooww? Muee meeeeoooww muee meeeeoooww?"

I shrugged with upturned hands. I carefully filled out the return merchandise form, including under Remarks: "Please refund my money as per your 'Money back guarantee if not satisfied.' " I boxed up the machine. Then I settled down for a nap.

Senior Year Notes

My first class Tuesday was English, my favorite because our teacher was crazy Ms. Velvet, a petite, dark-haired, classy and very cute girl not much older than we were. Some might say she acted somewhat younger. Most days she wore her rink-type roller skates. It was for efficiency, she told us.

I think she got started with the skating because she liked to play Duck, Duck, Goose. The desks were arranged in a circle. She would skate around behind us, having a great time and getting paid to be a teacher.

"Who wrote Of Time and the River?"

"Duck.....duck....duck....goose!"

The "goose" didn't chase her, just had to answer the question.

She had many aliases, because she changed her name each day. We had to guess from her outfit: Ms. Scarf, Ms. Bracelet, Ms.

Beauty Mark, Ms. Earrings, etc. She gave hints if we were stumped, like when she had a tiny squirrel pin or pinky ring. After somebody got it right, she'd write it on the board, and we were supposed to use her current alias. "My police record has supplement sheets," she told us.

This day she had on garish earrings. Kids said together: "Good Morning Ms. Earrings!" Too easy.

"One moment, Class, gotta keep my police record updated," said Ms. E.

She got out a pink PlaySkool desk phone and talked into it. "Hello, Ninth Precinct? Yes, Sarge, I'm calling again. I have another alias, Sophia Earrings, just add it on. What's that? A jewelry robbery, you say? That's awful!"

She had a box overflowing with toy jewels and sifted through it with her hand.

"What kind of jewels were they? Big diamonds, eh?" she said, picking up a huge plastic diamond.

"Why are you asking me about it? Ha, ha. I was home all evening. Like every evening. Are you married, Sarge? No? I don't suppose you like Polka dancing? No? Bowling? No? Roller skating? No? What's your name, 'Joe Friday'? I gotta go now."

We were going to be studying some works of Thomas Hardy. We went over some book reports on The Return of the Native and compared Hardy to other novelists. Went on for quite awhile.

Then she skated to the center of our little literary circle, and we all knew she was about to start her poetry speech.

She said, "Y'know, poetry has relevance, even though the poets are dead. By studying and reciting them we can bring those poems to life, even if we can't bring the poets to life."

Pause.

"Wait, maybe we <u>can</u> bring the poets to life! Has anyone <u>tried</u>?"

This was the cue for the room to be darkened. She pounded on the lid of the cardboard coffin in the center of the room, and Henry Longfellow stirred and stretched, asked for a glass of water and, by the light of a kerosene lantern, read "The Midnight Ride of Paul Revere".

Ms. Earrings thanked him. However, when he tried to climb out she closed down the lid on his fingers...

"No, no, that's all we have time for. Sorry."

....and piled some books on it. Pounding continued inside.

About then our principal, Mr. Chiarra, poked his head in the door, looked left and right, rolled his eyes, and left again.

****

"I'd love to get it working, Iggy," Dee Dee said, leaning a little closer to me with bright eyes and a gentle smile and of course I was in love with her. She was a knockout seventeen-year-old newly arrived at our high school and she charmed everybody. Normally the Dee Dee's of the world never talk to social zeroes like me, but it was happening, however briefly. This doesn't happen in real life, but it's happening in my story. Kvetchers are advised to write their own *&&^$% story. Mr. Skolnik let us use the lab area, and even gave us a key to the tool cabinet.

She brought this old shortwave radio the next day and we worked on it after school.

"Looks like these wires are pulled loose," I said, hoping that it was easy to fix, but then again wishing it would take hours, hours and hours, just me and Dee Dee, gorgeous Dee Dee....maybe we wouldn't give up, night after night, parts scattered, me explaining what superheterodyne meant, frequency modulation principles, Dee Dee sitting close and we would take breaks for coffee, and talk about life.

I re-soldered the wires and it suddenly worked. "Iggy, you did it!" she said, and she even gave me a little hug. Got any more radios, Dee?

We scanned through the channels and heard a police conversation:

"blxp...Center St ...building alarm...78 Center...the Minsky Factory.."

"My mom works there," said Dee. "I should get there to see if she's OK! It's two miles or so."

"We can go in my car," I offered.

"Iggy, you have a car? Let's go!"

We left the radio stuff and we went down to the first floor and out. Then Dee said, "Oh oh, I've got to go back, forgot my purse!"

Dee Dee came back pretty soon and said, "Let's go, I'll get it tomorrow.

"Iggy, it was scary! The lab light was back on and I peeked through the lab door window. Mr. Skolnik opened a <u>secret bookcase doorway</u>!

"Is this your car??? It looks like a golf cart."

"No, it's a King Midget, six-foot wheelbase and 4.5 HP engine, made from 1946 to 1969. My dad had it for years and then gave it to me."

"Iggy, I thought you had a real car, not a clown car! Hurry and start this crate, I don't want anybody to see me!"

I opened the engine hatch and pulled on the start cord.

"What are you dooooiiing?" She was laughing and holding her head.

"It's not electric start, you have to yank the pull cord."

Old Reliable got going and off we went, Dee Dee trying to crouch down, which was impossible. You were already crouched down, just riding.

"Don't tell anybody I rode in this, OK, pinky-promise?"

We curled pinkies and I said "Promise!"

"Dee Dee, isn't that a six-year-old girl thing?"

"Yes, so? You promised, now."

Dream Girl sat very close to me. Not because she wanted to, but because the little bench seat was narrow. I pretended she wanted to.

We got there and her mom was OK, not a big fire or anything.

"Thanks, Iggy, We'll talk tomorrow about Mr. S., the Mystery Man, OK?"

****

The next day was Wednesday. Ms. Velvet stepped off the cover of Glamour Magazine into our room, wearing red beads.

A chorus of "Good Morning, Ms. Beads!" was heard.

"One moment Class, she said, grabbing her toy phone. Her long fingers poked and jabbed at the phone keys, as though playing a few notes from Rachmaninoff. "Hello, Sarge, Yes, new alias, Brenda Beads. Slow day, is it? What? Not a burglary! In broad daylight! Oh, cameras, what else? Jewelry? Watches, huh?"

She fished in the jewelry box, picked up some toy watches, looked them over.

"Somebody saw a woman near Fox Jewelry Store, wearing red beads? Why are you telling me? Oh, I was home all day, or at

100

work, I never get to go out.

"Say, who's there with you? Only a prisoner? What's his name? Oh, I forgot, I've got to go teach some little kids, um, students. Bye."

We proceeded to a lot of discussion of the novel, The Great Gatsby. Questions back and forth.

Then she pointed to Norm as though he had raised his hand.

"Norm, did you have a question FOR ME?"

The "FOR ME" was the cue for the proposal routine.

"Yes, Ms. Beads, I've been meaning to ask you, will you marry me?"

"Norm, I thought you'd never ask!"

A pause. "One thing, Norm, when this question comes up, girls think about..." Here she looked at her hands and wiggled her fingers.

"Mittens?"

"No...."

"Fingernail polish?"

"No..."

"Baseball glove?"

"No…"

"A diamond engagement ring?"

"Yes!"

"Ms. Beads, I bought you one!" He tossed it and she caught it with a fielder's glove. She brought out an eye loupe, and studied the ring. She frowned, shaking her head "no".

"You know......, the marriage thing, I've thought about it a long time, but what with bond prices in Europe, and inflation, it just wouldn't work for us. Sorry.

"Of course, I'll return your ring, unless…maybe I could keep it to remember you by…."

"OK," Norm said.

"Thanks, it's so beautiful!" With that she tossed it into a box with about a hundred rings. Sometimes it goes on the floor, and she just waves her hand at it and never picks it up.

The poem for that day was "The Raven".

Mindy did a nice job of reading it. It was no surprise that Ms. Beads helped out in the presentation by playing the part of the raven in a bird suit with a yellow cardboard beak, standing behind Mindy and miming.

"While I nodded, nearly napping, suddenly there came a tapping,"

"BAM! BAM! BOOM!" Hammer blows on the door.

*"As of some one gently rapping, rapping at my chamber door.
'Tis some visitor,' I muttered, 'tapping at my chamber door' -"*

"BAM! BAM! BOOM!"

It seemed the raven got bored easily, yawning, reading a newspaper, smoking a cigar, gnawing on an ear of corn, preening, checking the time, reading a Woody Woodpecker comic, finally getting out a pillow and taking a nap.

The raven started to leave at the lines:

*"Leave my loneliness unbroken! - quit the bust above my door!
Take thy beak from out my heart, and take thy form from off my door!"*

But then came back because, as we know, the bird doesn't leave in the poem, 'nevermore' being an ostentatious way of saying 'never'. Personally, I think a whack with a broom would have solved the problem. That or a large cat.

****

Later that day Dee Dee and I went to the science lab. No one was around. Dee Dee pointed to the book case/hidden door. "He used this switch right here, and it popped open and he went in." It was one of those school light switches the janitors have a special key for.

"We need to get one of those keys, or make one," I said. "Why are we playing detective, anyway?"

"Beats classes, I guess," said Dee, "or a publishing company mistake has put us in a Nancy Drew Mystery."

I snooped around and cased the situation. I saw Dee Dee again and explained, "Mr. Bartleby, the janitor, has a little office in the furnace room. He keeps his keys on a wall rack, including the special light switch key."

Dee Dee said, "Listen, you hold Mr. Bartleby at gunpoint, while I grab the special key."

I said, "Wait, I didn't bring my gun."

Dee: "Hmm, better not make a career of this, if you can't remember to carry heat on a job."

We went with Plan "B". That was for Dee Dee to ask Mr. B. about the furnace and while he was distracted I would photograph the special key hanging on the key rack, then make one like it.

We went there. Dee Dee said, "Mr. Bartleby, we're studying combustion in science class. Will you show us how this big furnace works?"

"Sure, Young Lady, see, the coal from that big hopper there is fed by the feeder mechanism...."

While he explained, I took photos of the special key he had on the key rack and gave the "OK" sign to Dee Dee.

Mr. Bartleby was happy to show this cute girl all about the furnace.

"Now, would you like me to open the furnace door for a good

look at the combustion?"

Dee Dee said, "To be honest Mr. B., who cares? Let's go, Iggy."

"Thanks, Mr. B.," I said, and we left the puzzled janitor to carry on.

****

Ms. White Gloves was explaining parts of speech.

"Let's say you have the word 'charm' ....it can be a noun, as in 'the vivacious young teacher had <u>charm</u> to spare and was wise beyond her years'... or it can be a verb, as in 'the small-town girl <u>charmed</u> the handsome star of stage and....' " "Wait, did you hear a phone?...excuse me one..."

She picked up the play phone. "Hello,.....what's the name again? I'm kind of busy, y'know, you're (handsome movie star)? Uhmm, maybe I can talk a minute."

To us, covering the phone with her hand, "Some salesman, I'll get rid of him......"

"What's that? You saw a girl with white gloves?"

Ms. White Gloves looked at her white gloves.

"Am I the ravishing Dream Doll you saw?....."

She brought out a desktop mirror and checked her hair.

"....going into a shabby building, looks like a reform school?"

"Mr. (handsome movie star), now, how old would you say this young girl was?....About THIRTY-FIVE!!!??"

Ms. White Gloves fell off her chair and dropped the phone.

Sitting on the floor, she talked again. "This mystery girl, you saw her from a long way away? Like, I mean far?....no, walked right by you, huh? Oh... you have another call from... (famous beautiful actress)? oh ...I heard a click, are you still there? Hello? Hello?

"Kids, it never pays to talk to salesmen. Now, let's knock off another curriculum item!"

We did. Curriculum Item 27, Comic Opera. She brought out the comic "Dipsilla Duck and the Mystery of the Opera".

"We'll do a reading right here in class. Here's a hat with slips of paper, one for each part. Not enough parts for everybody. Don't cry if you get a blank. We'll blast through it in no time."

There was a push for costumes or at least yellow duck beaks. Drama club members argued that they might not feel ducky enough to really project their characters. Sorry, no time, ruled Ms. W. G.

There was some raggedness since we had to jam in a bunch and pass around the single pasted-up copy of the comic book. In the story, Dulcimeria fills in for Dipsilla Duck, a famous (in Lower Duckbeak Falls) opera singer who had a hangover or something. Deenie was Dulcimeria, but didn't know the aria Fantuichio d'Amouri, so she sang "Three Little Fishies" instead, to much applause.

I was the police inspector, and was glad to get a pretty important part. In the comic he looked like a dog, so I growled my part just a bit.

(Spoiler Alert) You will be glad to know that the evil criminals were unmasked and apprehended. They turned out to be ermine who cleverly disguised themselves as ducks, those weasels! You see, first they made friends with the night janitor at the opera house, and.... oh, never mind.

****

"We'll work together on this," Dee said to me. "But one thing, if we need to talk, signal by slapping at mosquitoes, then we'll meet by the vending machines when nobody's around."

I made a duplicate switch key out of a fork from the cafeteria. Yes, I am clever that way. I tested it quickly at lunchtime. Success! The high glass bookcase opened. I closed it again. Now we would wait for a chance to see what we could see.

Late in the afternoon Dee Dee was in the hall surrounded by friends gabbing high school chit chat. I went to my locker and gave the signal by slapping at imaginary bugs. "SLAP!" She didn't seem to notice. "SLAP! SLAP!" Ms. Velvet came over and started slapping and jumping up to get high ones, then two other kids did, too. Ms. Velvet said, "Hold still. SMACK!" on top of my head. "Hold still, he's right there! SMACK! SMACK! There he is! SMACK!"

"They've gone now! They've gone now!" I said as I made my getaway.

"Glad to help," said Ms. V. with a big smirk. A lot of laughter.

Very funny, guys.

Later, by the vending machines, I said, "We can get in now, but when is it safe to try it?"

"He's gotta go home sometime, we'll just wait until he leaves for the day, then we scoot in and discover what he's hiding."

We hung around in a study hall room and saw him get in his car and leave at about 5:00 PM. Dee pulled out a credit card and jimmied open the lab door.

"Are you a professional criminal, Dee Dee?"

"Alas, still an amateur."

The bent fork worked as before, opening the secret door and in we went, climbing down a ladder.

We gaped at a fantastic sight! In the center of the room was a flying saucer!

It was ten feet in diameter and had a pilot's seat in the center. Under construction? Or being taken apart?

"Mr. Skolnik is a crazy man building a flying saucer!"

"Or an alien planning to take over Hannibal High School!"

"Y'know, Mr. S. does act funny sometimes, the way he walks …reminds me of a duck."

"Yeees, could be an outer space duck wearing a human mask….he scratches his little beard all the time, does his mask itch?"

It was a big basement room loaded with equipment shelves and tools. Big garage door to the outside apparently kept locked.

Suddenly we heard voices upstairs. "Shhhh." We hid behind the shelves in the shadows.

"Clump, clump, clump." Mr. S. and another man.

"Looks impressive, Siegfried, but will it fly? Heh, heh."

"Soon, soon, Mr. (famous billionaire). I'm having just a little trouble tuning the megawatt laser, the frequency keeps moving into the red."

"Hah, your whole &^^$$% operation is in the red, Siegfried! Explain again why this crate is supposed to fly."

"OK, remember, it's secret, no telling. In 1890 H.G. Wells's brother had a theory that there was such a thing as anti-gravity material, gravity in reverse, and there is a lot of it even on earth, but once it comes to the surface it is repelled straight up, whoosh into space, so naturally nobody finds it. But it can be found in caves, on the roofs of caves.

"In fact, bats eat this material and it makes them lighter.

"Through many experiments I found out how to convert ordinary starch to anti-gravity starch. I bombard corn kernels with a special laser and it will flip to become anti-gravity starch!

"Then I put it into the lift chamber of my vehicle and it will be carried into space, no rockets required!

"I am waiting right now to see if the new batch of material is good, it takes awhile to ripen, you see, after the laser treatment. It is in the vehicle now, we shall see.

"Mr. (famous billionaire), I only need a little more money, to replace the expendables, you know…"

"Oh, Good Grief, here it comes…"

"It's $39.50 for a Griswald twombee, and new snap gaskets would be $5.99 each,…"

"It will have to wait until I review my financial status. I'm expecting two billion, or is it three billion, tomorrow in dividends. I'll let you know. Give me a call if that anti-gravity popcorn starts floating."

We could hear them going up the ladder. "You're not pals with those cold fusion guys are you?"

"CLONK!" the bookcase door closed, and the lights all turned out, also.

We were crouched together all this time. Oooh sooo close!

Dee Dee said, "It's pitch black! Let's get out of here!" We crept toward the exit.

"Hold my hand, Iggy. I'm not scared of the dark, Iggy, you understand."

Now, it was her idea, holding hands, really. We got outside the building without being seen. It was pretty dark by then.

"How fantastic, real crazy guy."

"About Mr. S., should we report him? Maybe the school knows anyway, he's just using some space in the cellar. I don't know what we should do."

"Want a ride home?" I asked. Ever courteous, I am.

"In your cramped little tin car? I only live two blocks from here."

"Funny thing is, I like being cramped with you."

"Iggy, Iggy, remember, we're not <u>going</u> together....we're just .... <u>conspiring</u> together."

"Oh yeah, OK. Goodnight."

****

On Friday, English was taught by Ms. Diamond, the conse-quence of the outsized plastic diamond the teacher wore.

"One moment," she said. "That's the phone." She answered the PlaySkool phone which wasn't ringing.

"Hi, (famous movie star)!" she said in a bright voice. Then, "I'm sorry about driving your Ferrari into the pond,....they didn't find it yet?...oh,...too bad. But (famous movie star), it's not like I do this <u>all</u> the time.....Yes, there was the Red Maserati....What? Our engagement is.....off? Oh, all right. The ring? Oh sure, of course I'll send it back. Bye." Then she

111

took off the ring and dropped it in her box with the other hundred rings.

Sitting down, she said, head in hands, "Give me a minute, OK? Sniff." She brought out a hanky and put it up to her eyes and squeezed water out of it which dripped down her face onto some papers on the desk. Then, "Some of your homework got a little wet. Sorry, sniff." Then from a hidden pan of water, she brought up sopping wet papers and put them on the radiator. Some went on the floor, but she pretended not to notice.

Now it was time for some literature studies. As she talked, she made a necklace out of some of her engagement rings and paper clips.

"I presume you've all read the novel we're going to analyze, Ms. Dove Takes Flight."

Ms. Diamond continued, "Class, I'll summarize the novel to get us started. It tells in graceful prose the poignant and thrilling story of an English teacher of dazzling beauty who starts her career modestly at a run-down dump of a school at a meager salary. The other teachers are dim bulbs. Her students sometimes don't do their assignments, handing in theme papers of gibberish. They rhyme orange with porridge which is horridge, I mean horrid.

"Her talents are wasted at the backwater school. Undaunted, she progressively succeeds and is voted best in every category of her profession. Yet inside, this person yearns for far greater glories. She skillfully hides her broken heart with outward mirth, sometimes even making a joke as she carries on her serious duties.

"Her thorough study of thousands of famous works of literature makes her aware of how feeble those efforts have been. In her spare time she writes 50 novels, and they are acclaimed and published. Of course, modesty prevents this genius from taking any credit; she uses a pen name for all. She spends her vast fortune from these on advancing her unique philosophy of living, which she calls 'Velvetism'. Also, she discusses her method of raising earthworms for fun and profit.

"The publishers tell us that a sequel is in the works, which will cover the many much greater accomplishments she has since attained. She writes under the pen name 'Tevlev'.

"Class, next time we'll continue with <u>Ms. Dove Takes Flight</u>, it's such a great book, I've read it over and over!

Pause.

"Oops, I got mixed up, of course we're reading <u>Good Morning, Miss Dove</u>.

At the end of class, Dee Dee waved me over to talk in a corner of the room.

"Iggy, help me play a little joke on Ms. Velvet. We need two Keystone Kops uniforms from the Drama Department."

"Easy," I said, "I have a key to the prop room."

****

Later in the day Dee Dee and I were in Mr. Skolnik's science class. He was droning on and on. After class I talked to Dee

Dee. Wouldn't it be fun to do a big demonstration of the conservation of angular momentum using skaters?

In a gym or big space a center person pulls in a rope attached to a skater while the skater coasts in a circle, and then goes faster and faster as the rope gets shorter.

"Good idea, Iggy. Of course, we know one skater who can skate backwards playing Duck, Duck, Goose!"

Ms. V. agreed to help. It was late in the day and Mr. Skolnik had left when the three of us came back to the lab.

"We'll talk to him tomorrow," said Ms. Velvet. "We'll need a long rope or clothesline. Come on in the lab, I know where there's some rope."

Teachers have keys, so we went right in. She went over and used a light switch key and opened the secret door!

"Ms. Velvet! You know about the secret room!"

"You kids knew about it? Hah! I'm not surprised, really, lots of people know it's here, but old Fuddy-Duddy thinks it's his big secret space, him and his anti-gravity craziness! Alvin goes there to help, too, I know. There's some rope down there, I'll go get it."

Dee Dee said, "Listen, I just thought of a cute little joke. Iggy, remember Mr. S. said the anti-gravity popcorn didn't show it's properties right away?"

"It's perfect. We'll use some ropes to pull his contraption up to the ceiling. When he goes down there he'll think at last his

114

stupid popcorn is working, at least until he discovers the ropes!"

It only took a few minutes to attach it overhead to some ceiling pipes. It was a pretty light spaceship. Then three chortling pranksters sneaked away into the night.

****

Mr. Skolnik arrived the next morning as usual. He may have wondered why Ms. Velvet, Dee Dee and I were hanging around nonchalantly outside his lab.

I peered with one eye through the little classroom door window. Aha! He quickly disappeared through the secret door!

He immediately reappeared and came bursting back out past us and went to the school office. We could see him on the phone.

"Perfect," said Ms. Velvet. She let us in and we went down the ladder, lowered the saucer contraption back down, hid the ropes, and came back. Mr. Skolnik was still on the phone.

Dee Dee was giggling like a schoolgirl. She was a schoolgirl, of course.

Ms. Velvet giggled. I did not giggle, I went, "Heh, heh, hee, hee." in a manly way.

A very happy Mr. Skolnik came back our way. We were awkwardly standing around.

"Ms. Velvet, Dee Dee, Iggy, please come with me. Something

wonderful has happened and it's been secret for some time, but now it can be revealed! General Bufinox will soon be here, also."

As we climbed down the ladder, I felt guilty.

I said, "Mr. Skolnik, I hope you won't be mad at me. I played a trick on you, lifted your spaceship with ropes, as a joke, but I'm sorry….it was kind of mean."

"What are you saying, joke?" asked Mr. Skolnik.

We climbed down the ladder and the spaceship was back up at the ceiling!!

The three of us pranksters blinked in disbelief. Mr. S. pushed and pulled as the little ship floated. He pulled down on one side and it bobbed back up like a helium balloon, but with much greater force.

Mr. Skolnik was fairly dancing with excitement. General Bufinox arrived and Mr. Skolnik went on and on, showing and explaining.

Dear Reader, you may wonder why you have heard nothing of this scientific breakthrough. The answer is very simple: the government doesn't want you to know about it! They will tell you that what you are reading here is a silly little story.

****

Dee Dee and I didn't go in at first to the next English class. We hovered at the door in our cop uniforms and peeked through the window. Then just as Ms. Velvet (Ms. Tiara, that day) was on the toy phone and riffling through the fake jewels, we dramatically burst into the room.

"Young Lady, we'd like to talk to you about those jewels!" I said authoritatively.

"Why, whatever do you mean, Officers?" she said, in a velvety Scarlett O'Hara voice.

"Oh, these? I wondered where these came from. Somebody must have carelessly left them here. Of course you could check for fingerprints to find out...."

This while she hurriedly wiped all over the plastic box with the crying hanky.

Dee Dee said, "There have been several robberies and we have detailed descriptions....your thieving days are over, Ducky!"

"The long arm of the law has arrived!" I added.

Then suddenly, Ms. Tiara covered her face with her hands. "It's no use!" she sniffed. Fake tears dripped down her face from the crying hanky.

She said, "Norm, (sniff) we'll have to postpone our wedding. I'll be in the big house. Wait, I flipped you off, I forgot."

Then I said, suddenly sympathetic, "Well, Ma'am, if you're going to cry....never mind. It's Ok, Stop crying. Keep the silly jewels."

Dee Dee said, "There, there, here, just keep them,... we don't want to do the paperwork anyway."

We put our arms around her, and patted her head. Then out we went.

We shed the uniforms and came back into class. "Sorry we're late."

Ms. Tiara said, "Did you see two cops out there? What patsies they were!"

****

I was getting a drink from the corridor fountain when someone came close. I looked up. It was Dee Dee.

"Graduation in a few days, Iggy. I can't believe time went by so fast," she said. "Y'know, I've got some sort-of boyfriends here, but they're all kind of yokels. Don't tell anybody I said that. I hope for better pickin's at the rinky-dink college I'm going to. Do I sound like a scheming woman? I am. Oh, oh, people coming, seeya, Iggy."

****

"Final papers ready in the office, Iggy," said Ms. Velvet, looking as beautiful as ever. She adjusted her silk scarf and looked this way and that. "Well, you graduate later today, congratulations."

"Iggy, teachers are not supposed to fraternize with students, but tomorrow will be a different story. How about a ride in your King Midget? We could go to a drive-in movie or something."

"I thought you'd never ask!" I said.

The Quantrill Gang

I was heading up FBI Crime Team Eleven when the call came in: paper clips and rubber bands missing at the big DELETED plant in DELETED. Prime suspects: The notorious Quantrill Gang.

I won't bore you with stuff about how I got to lead FBI Crime Team Eleven, well, maybe a little about it. I was in the car maintenance field in New Orleans, DELETED, DELETED Service Station, in the French Quarter. I worked my way up for ten years on the job. I was pretty much the go-to man for tire-changing.

One day I happened to be reading a Dipsilla Duck comic and right there in the back was the ad: "FBI Career! Send For Details." I mailed in my application and then there was the long wait. I was accepted! I took their complete $37.50 course. That was the Premium Course. Had to go to DELETED, DELETED, for the handcuffs lessons and how to knock any attacker down methods.

And you know the rest of the story- they did hire me! You could say I got in on the ground floor....mostly sweeping, then they trained me on the floor polisher! The type I ran was a French machine, the Floor-Dee-Lee.

Quantrill, Quantrill, the name kept coming up and when we pieced some things together, a picture emerged: several gang members, hard cases, had infiltrated the big DELETED car assembly plant in DELETED. They were in deep cover there biding time, up to no good we were sure. Was there a connection with the missing paper clips? My assignment: Deploy nineteen seasoned agents to go undercover as emp-loyees at the DELETED plant, and wait for this nefarious cabal to make their next move!

You probably know, when you are undercover, you have to use a number of subterfuges to avoid detection. For example, we all had code names, and pretended not to know each other, even though we were a tight-knit team and did know each other or at least had heard of each other. First thing, I called a secret midnight beach meeting, or SMBM, a common method to avoid eavesdropping, to make our plans. (Not to be confused with ICBM, which means DELETED, DELETED, DELETED, DELETED and is not something Crime Team Eleven would normally use.) It was then I handed out the white slips of paper with the code name to each of my team.

"Memorize your code name, and then we'll burn these in this fire." I had thoughtfully prepared a nice fire on the beach and brought some marshmallows, too.

'Course, nothing is easy, one young lady, can't tell you her name, had cheeks like a squirrel. Didn't want the code name

"Chipmunk". Another person didn't like the code name "Bozo". "Olive Oyl" didn't want that name. He said it wasn't dignified. "It's just a secret name, Folks!" I said, "your friends and family, they won't know, just us FBI people."

Well, with all the complaints I said, "OK, I don't care what these names are, think up your own and then you'll be happy!" So they all liked that and started in thinking. But....there happened to be that we had identical twins on the team, and they picked "Tweedle-Dum" and "Tweedle-Dee" for their secret names. I said, if those words are used around the plant, it might be a hint, you know.

Elizabeth came to me and wanted the code name "Liz" and I explained that she was a dimwit, wasn't she? She pouted. For some reason reindeer names were popular, three requests for "Blitzen". Two of the guys (not big guys) wanted "Rambo".

"Oh Heck, you can't have duplicates, People!"

We hadn't settled on a thing, not one single code name, when the local DELETED Police Department car pulls up right on the beach sand, with his blinky lights.

"Sorry, Folks, fires aren't allowed, here. Don't you read signs?"

He was a tubby guy with his hands on his belt, kind of officious, don't you think?

Well, I could have pulled rank, I suppose; Federal FBI business trumps pipsqueak DELETED petty beach rules, you know? But one of the things they teach in FBI school is don't get arrested and get your names in the paper when you are doing undercover work.

He stomped out our fire with his big boots and we never even got to the marshmallow roasting I had planned.

Disappointments and danger are all part of working for The Company. Or is that the CIA?

Well, my superior got on me, so I directed the team to report to the DELETED plant forthwith. We'd have to set up the code names on the fly. Listen, in this business you have to roll in the punch.

It was all fixed with the plant General Manager, Grimley Stanford III, to get us all hired, even though none of us knew diddly about the car business. We just waltzed in and the regular, real employees were thinking: "Who the &^%$%^ are all these dumb bunnies showing up, anyway, just hanging around?" That was kind of a weakness of the plan.

Headquarters set up a private courier system, phones not being secure enough. It was a good plan. Messages would be delivered by a DELETED Ice Cream truck. All we had to do was go out and ask for a special ice cream that only we knew about, then the message would be hidden in the ice cream bar.

Tuesday. Everybody at work, our second day. Cars are coming down the long line, Man, they move fast. Butch, in a sweat, is doing engine installation. "Get outta my &%$#%%$ way, Twinkie!!!" he says. I guess he's talking to me.

I hear a bell outside. It's the ice cream truck. "I'll be right back, Butch," I say, pleasantly.

"&%$%#& you!" he says.

I'm at the truck: "One Dilly-Dally Bar, please."

Got back inside. Now to read the message. I ducked behind a curtain area and start to open the Dilly-Dally Bar. Blinding bright flashes from arc welding! "Get the &$%$##$ out of my booth, Dingbat!!" said the welding employee.

I dropped the ice cream and it went splat on the floor as I left in a hurry. Then I tried to reach back in but he saw me and stomped my ice cream with his steel-toe. A spiteful person! However, he went back to his miserable welding job and I carefully retrieved the message paper.

It said: "FBI Crime Team Eleven Volleyball sign-up sheet is now posted in the DELETED Cafeteria. Destroy after reading."

Things were falling into place. I quickly chewed up the paper and swallowed it. (Actually it wasn't bad, needed salt maybe, but would have that healthy fiber content.) Then it was on to the code names for my team. I went down the line to Grace. (Remember, all names have been changed for this document.)

"Hi Grace, I don't know you, of course, but I understand your name is Grace. Glad to meet you. What did you decide about ode-co ame-nay? You can write it here on this little card." I went wink, wink, wink with my eyes.

"My kokomo manay? What the &%$$#% are you talking about?"

"You know, in other words C. N. for.....?" I pointed at her.

"Oh, code name? I think 'Blitzen' is good."

"Sssshhhh!"

I had equal success with the other team members. Finally we were ready to gather intelligence regarding the Quantrill Gang (Code name: "Gravediggers").

Lunch break. I sat with Elizabeth (Prancer) and Dale (Wolf). I introduced myself. Heh, heh, never saw these people before, heh, heh!

"Hear any interesting news about Gravediggers?" I asked, cryptically.

"Listen, Cinderella told me she thinks she knows one of the Gravediggers, it's the ZZZT ZZZT, spark, spark guy."

Now we're getting somewhere. I gave this person the code name "Scumbag".

Wednesday. A breakthrough! Marmalade saw Scumbag writing in a diary! He keeps it hidden, under his bench. We have to get access to that diary!

It's midnight, dark. All is quiet, there's no third shift at this plant. Vixen and I look under the bench. He's got a little combination safe!

Luckily, FBI standard equipment includes an electronic safe opener called the Crack-O-Matic™ (As advertised on TV). We bust the safe and read his diary.

Latest entries:

Dear Diary, Man, my head hurts...these &%$#%^ welding fumes!!! &^%$%% &&^^%$, ...(here we leave out a few paragraphs of complaints about health, his gun moll, etc)...

...Warts has things lined up, what we'll do is, he passes the paper clips and the stapler to me, and I'll hide them in the front passenger door panel. Then when the car gets to the destination, our boss Whitey just opens it up when nobody's looking! It'll be the Mauve DELETED DELETED, central antenna, sun roof option, fake wire hubcaps!

"Ulp!" I exclaim. "They've got a stapler, too! "

All we have to do now is follow that car and nab the mysterious Whitey when he unscrews the door panel.

Next day. Cars going down the line and out the door. There it is! Mauve DELETED. I quickly enlist Houdini and Lobster and we run after the car as they drive it to the holding area. If Whitey shows up, I'll rush in with Lobster and we'll pinch the mobster!

In shifts we watch the car all day. About 1:00 AM, it's pitch dark...a figure emerges from the shadows and quickly opens the car door. In seconds he has the door panel removed. Now I give a signal and we move in.

He is startled as I shine the light on him. He wears a natty white suit and blue tie. He's taking out the paper clips and stuffing them hurriedly into a gunny sack...he doesn't look like a common criminal....no, indeed, it's none other than Mr. Grimley Stanford III, the manager of the entire DELETED

DELETED plant!

"Stealing from your own plant, eh, Mr. Stanford? Very clever, no one in the world would suspect YOU!

"Now we know YOU are the boss of the Quantrill Gang! No wonder your Boys could easily infiltrate the plant."

We could tell, as he furtively shifted his eyes, he was thinking of making a break for it. He changed his mind as he stared down the barrel of my Glock .45 automatic. Houdini brought out his handcuffs and we took Mr. Big into custody.

How "Bird" Daffodil Got His Name

Dr. Bleakness, making his morning rounds, checked the new patient. He was a minor league pitcher, still in a coma the day after being hit on the head by a line drive.

He seemed to be sleeping comfortably. The patient in the bed next to him changed the channel on the TV. The zookeeper host was then showing a Carter's Grosbeak, whose call was "Weeeech-chee-chee! Weeeech-chee-chee!"

The young patient stirred, opened his eyes and said, "WEEEECH-CHEE-CHEE! WEEEECH-CHEE-CHEE!" He looked around nervously, and scrambled out of the bed and pressed against the window, and flapped his arms. Failing to fly through the window glass, he hopped down the hall until being led back to his room by burly orderlies.

"An unusual case. Mr. Daffodil thinks he is a bird and so is afraid of any animal which could be an enemy," said Dr. Bleakness at the Floor Summary Meeting.

Phil Daffodil calmed down after a while. He still thought he was a bird, but acted like a tame bird. He had a disconcerting tendency to say, "WEEEECH-CHEE-CHEE! WEEEECH-CHEE-CHEE!" quite loudly, but otherwise conversed normally and so was sent home.

His wife advised everyone she knew about the situation. "Phil got hit on the head and thinks he's a bird. Just humor him, please."

His team manager, Mr. Casey, said, "I don't care if he thinks he's a bird, as long as he's a bird that throws fastballs."

"My head is still sore, otherwise I generally feel fine, but I think I need to see Benny, my tailor," Phil said to his wife, Sally.

Always a natty dresser, Daffodil had several quality suits, but they no longer felt right at all. He took one of his suits to Benny. "Just won't do, Benny, it's too tight, not full enough, not....feathery enough."

"Feathery? You ain't a bird, what's with 'feathery'?"

"But Benny, I am a bird, a Carter's Grosbeak."

"Yeah, and I'm the King of Spain. You want to look like a bird, try Fantasy Costumes, Tenth Street."

Benny had good advice, and Phil returned home wearing a handsome bird outfit, with gray and white feathers and a huge beak. The eyes were clear plastic so Phil could see pretty well.

"Sally, this is more like it! I feel better."

Phil was a cigar smoker, and the beak got in the way some, but he bought longer cigars and that helped.

Not feeling so comfortable in his old house, Phil spent several days building a huge nest of branches up in the thick woods behind his house. Thanks to careful research about grosbeaks, he expertly wove slender branches into a fine nest about 10 feet in diameter. It was high above the ground, safe from foxes.

His teammates and manager greeted him on his return to practice with them.

He soon demonstrated that the accident had taken nothing off his blazing fastball.

****

Meanwhile, one Thaddeus Thistle, Town Manager of Uppity Falls, stared at his computer screen. Apparently Google Maps had new aerial views of his town. Or maybe he hadn't noticed it before. But he noticed it now. Clearly something unusual has been constructed in the rear area of 326 Pinehurst Drive. It looked like a huge round unkempt bundle of brush and sticks. And if it was unusual, surely it was a violation of some of the tangled web of town regulations, ordinances, and prohibitions, and must be dealt with.

At present, though, it was time for his Monday morning meeting with his top echelon. He quickly assembled the group in a small conference room, closed the door, and stood before them.

"We have a new member in our group this morning, Mr. Calvin Stonewall.

"As you may know, Cal, some goody-two-shoes in the previous administration, l'ancien régime, instituted the sappy town motto 'Do Good' and you see this on our stationery and so forth.

"Not to be outdone, I instituted a 'Do Good' Group, as you see here. We get together in private for a little discussion on Mondays."

He drew the window shades down, then wrote on the white board "D.O. G.O.O.D."

"What does it stand for?" He answered his own question, pointing to each letter:

"Deny, Obstruct, Grind down, Overrule, Oppose, Delay.

"All together, now!"

All responded: "DENY! OBSTRUCT! GRIND DOWN! OVERRULE! OPPOSE! DELAY!"

"We have a 'Do Good' gesture, what is it?"

All gave a thumbs down sign.

"And what do we say as we present the 'Do Good' gesture?"

All: "Noooooo!"

"I think that about sums up my remarks this morning, Let's get some coffee.

"Geraldine, let's talk about how we'll ram through that pension increase for all hands."

The phone was ringing when they came out and Cal took the call.

"Boss, it's from the Widow Cialdini. She wants to have a yard sale…"

"Explain the license required, the insurance, the bond posting, the inspection requirements, the three environmental impact statements, the traffic control plan, and the rest. Remember our motto 'Do Good', heh, heh, heh."

Boss Thistle's attention returned to the offending branch cluster.

A "Notice of Violation" letter went out to Mr. Phil Daffodil stating that his round construction of branches must be taken down because it was in violation of town ordinances. This was known in the department as "Bluff Letter No. 1", since it didn't specify what ordinance was being violated. It was called a bluff because many times there was no such ordinance.

However, Ms. Daffodil was a trial lawyer and not so easily bluffed. She replied that they would be happy to comply if the town would explain what town ordinance was being violated.

The town sent "Bluff Letter No. 2", which was the same, but more threatening. "Bluff Letter No. 3" didn't work either.

Thistle's lackeys spent days and found nothing pertaining to this wayward Daffodil activity. It seems nothing prevented a man from assembling sticks into a giant nest on his property in the town of Uppity Falls.

Not one to back away from a fight, Thistle gathered his bureaucratic underlings and whipped up a new ordinance, effective immediately, requiring nests to be no larger than <u>one foot in diameter</u>.

A notice of this was put in the mail to the Daffodils.

****

It was a beautiful summer day, birds were singing in the trees, and butterflies were around and about. One very large bird was singing, too, "WEEEECH-CHEE-CHEE! WEEEECH-CHEE-CHEE!". Phil was out for a drive to enjoy some fresh air. If you have ever driven a car in a bird suit, you'd know how the darned wings get in the way. This happened to Phil. As he turned a corner, his wing caught the steering wheel and he went into the ditch and on into a cornfield full of ripe, tall stalks. Unhurt, he got out and surveyed the situation.

Just then an old sputtering truck came down the dusty road and slowed and stopped. Jean Paul Fermat, a farmer, got out.

"Hey!" he said.

Like any farmer with a big bird in his cornfield, he was unhappy. He had an old truck, but a new cell phone. He called the Sheriff's Office.

"Some bird drove into my cornfield, and I want him arrested! Hurry up before he tries to git away."

"That Mr. Fermat again," said the Duty Officer. Reluctantly he drove the Dixie Special over to the scene of the alleged crime.

"Well, Mr. Bird, you been at some party or somethin'? Mr. Fermat says you drove into his corn. That right?" asked the deputy.

A big blue jay flew overhead just then. "WEEEECH-CHEE-CHEE! WEEEECH-CHEE-CHEE!" said Phil. "Sorry, Officer, that was a rival bird and I warned him off."

"I got a suspicion you've been drinkin', early in the day, too. A man that drinks at noon, he's got a problem."

"Sir, I'm not a man, I'm a bird, a Carter's Grosbeak, and I seldom drink. Well, does beer count?"

"Yer a bird, eh? Sir, I'm gonna have to give you a Breathalyzer test."

Phil put the device in his beak and breathed out. Of course, not much breath went through the round tube. It showed no alcohol in his breath.

"It ain't working 'cause of your big beak. %$^&*#, here, I want you to try to walk a straight line, instead!" The deputy scratched a long line in the dirt.

"OK, Officer," said the suspect. He proceeded to hop along the line, more or less straight.

"I said walk, not hop!"

"Sir, I can't help it if I'm a Carter's Grosbeak. We don't walk, we hop."

"OK, I'm putting you down as 'uncooperative' and taking you in. Sir, put your wings behind you, gotta cuff you."

At the lockup, they put Phil in Cell No.1 with an inebriated gentleman who was asleep. He awoke and blinked, observing the six-foot tall Carter's Grosbeak sitting in the cell.

"Guard, guard, they's a bird in my cell, a really big one, my Gawd, get him out. How'd he get in?"

"We arrested him."

"You arrestin' birds now? It ain't right....birds should be free."

Luckily, the sheriff knew Phil and the whole story of him getting beaned and knew he wasn't drunk. They let him go.

His cellmate said, "That's more like it. Why dontcha go arrest some &^%%$ squirrels, now!?"

****

Phil's wife read the notice of the new town ordinance, observing with interest the words, "...nests to be no larger than one foot in diameter."

Ms. Daffodil, no shrinking violet, immediately phoned a friend in the higher levels of an organization known for its vigorous defense of wildlife. She explained the reckless actions of the town bigwigs, summarizing, "I'm sure you would agree that we must protect our wildlife from meddling town bureaucrats." Her friend did agree. Philadelphia lawyers were contacted.

A communication soon landed on Mr. Thistle's desk from the offices of Courtney, Finegold, and Penn, Attorneys at Law:

The Town of Uppity Falls may want to reconsider its new unlawful attempt to regulate wildlife nests. Clearly this sloppily written regulation illegally interferes with the following:
U.S. Code June 28, 1930, ch. 709, § 1,46 Stat. 827, ***Wildlife Habitats, Measurements Allowed.***

U.S. Code May 18, 1948, ch. 303, § 1,62 Stat. 238, ***Flying Creatures, Observation of.***

U.S. Code July 3, 1958, ch. 456, §1,67 Stat. 216, ***Migrating Wildlife, Safe Shelter Preservation.***

U.S. Code Dec 19, 1970, ch. 539, §1,26 Stat. 750, ***Tree-dweller's Privacy Preservation.***

While perusing the hodgepodge known as "Uppity Falls Town Guide", one of our legal interns noted that 19 sections were ***illegal*** *because of violating Federal and State of DELETED law as follows:*

Section I, Subheading 3, Leaves, Disposal of ....Viol. of Pub. L. 87-543, §3, Aug. 7, 1958, 72 Stat. 479, ***Twig Recycling.***

Section II, Subheading 9, Sidewalk Clearing....Viol. of U.S. Code Dec 29, 1980, ch. 839, §1,16 Stat. 540, ***Acceptable Frozen Water Transport Methods.***

Section II, Subheading 5, Lemonade and Roadside Stands,

Bookkeeping Requirements....Viol. of U.S. Code July 6, 1968, ch. 436, §1,61 Stat. 746 **Generally Accepted Accounting Practices, Applicability and Schedules.**

Section II, Subheading 4, Driveways, Cracks and Weeds Limitations....Viol. of U.S. Code July, 1948, ch. 416, §1,21 Stat. 733, **Weed Protection Protocols***.*

Section III, Subheading 2, Stumps, Removal Requirements.... Viol. of Pub. L. 87-532, §2, Aug. 12, 1978, 72 Stat. 669, **Rotten Wood, Encouragement of,**

and 13 others we haven't the time to list here because of pressing business before the U.S. Supreme court. Please see attached detailed list.

No doubt you will immediately correct these blatant illegalities, so that we may avoid the unpleasantness and expense of lawsuits by persons, institutions, and branches of government having standing in these cases.

Interestingly, some of these potential cases appear to be quite similar to DELETED v. Beswick, 283 Vt. 2d 780 (1989). Mr. Beswick, who was formerly the Town Manager of DELETED, DELETED was responsible for town regulations pertaining to handling of fishing bait which were held to be damaging to and interfering with DELETED State Code Sect. 7, Chapter 78, **Worm Harvesting Length Requirements.** *After he was released from prison, Mr. Beswick unfortunately was unable to find gainful employment and his present whereabouts are unknown to us. Note enclosed photo of Mr. Beswick, which accompanied the (a famous newspaper) article titled: "DELETED Homeless: Will They Survive the Winter?" Mr. Beswick is third from the left, holding the tin cup.*

*You might be interested to know that our organization is considering a program to teach wildlife awareness, whereby scout groups and school children build **giant nests** in trees, with big prizes for the largest and other categories. Uppity Falls would be a good choice for the kickoff of this effort. Please let us know if your town is interested in supporting the above initiative.*

After reading the above, Town Manager Thistle took some deep breaths and held his head between his hands.

"Boss, we're ready now with this second warning letter to the Daffodils; this'll put some fear into 'em."

"Snively, hold off on that for now."

****

Relieved to be out of the jail, Phil trekked toward home, which wasn't really very far. He came to a rambling establishment labeled "DELETED Feed and Seed" and entered.

The slumped clerk at the counter eyed him suspiciously.

"Howdy, I'd like this 30 lb bag of bird seed right here. But I don't have money on me. No pockets, see, money's in my car, but I ran off the road, haven't got back to it yet, see? Can I take it and bring money later?"

The clerk stepped into the back.

"Boss, there's a goofy-looking bird out here wants to buy seed on credit."

137

"Do you recognize him?"

"I'd say he's a grackle, or a starling, but he's gray, not black."

"Remember the Cardinal Rule: If we don't recognize 'em, no credit!"

Having no luck there, Phil continued on. He soon arrived home and reported an important discovery:

"Sally, Sally, look! I found this egg as I went by the park. It must have fallen out of a nest."

"Phil, that's a beach ball."

"No, no, Sally, it's an oriole egg, I think. Listen, we'll try to find the mother, but we have to protect it and hatch it. I'll put it in our nest right away. We might even adopt the chick, you know, since we have no little ones of our own."

Phil climbed up and tucked the beach ball in the nest, and covered it with a small blanket.

"Should be safe from predators hid under a blanket. Gotta keep it warm by sitting on it, too, if we expect it to hatch."

"Phil, we've been invited to the Fox's for a dinner party tonight. Do you want to go? Dan Wolf and his wife will be there, too. You like them, don't you? It'll be fun."

"Whoa, the Fox's?" asked Phil, starting to perspire a little. "Do we have to? You know, it ain't that I'm afraid...but I mean a fox and a wolf inviting me, a grosbeak, for dinner?

"No, no, he's not a real fox, it's just a name. We've been there before, you remember, don't you?"

"Hmmm, yeah, yeah,..I know Harvey Fox, yeah," said Phil.

"It'll be fun. Cindy's having roast turkey and it's a big one so they started cooking the bird this afternoon."

"Gulp...they cooked a BIRD???" said Phil.

"Phil, Phil, now, it'll be OK. Listen, Harvey loves baseball, remember? You can talk about pitching, and fielding, and the infield fly rule, whatever that is."

"See, Hon, let's say there's a pop-up with men on base, see...."

"Yes, you explained it before, but I still don't understand it. And there's that thing about if the bat-boy gets in the way, that Cindy brought up.

"If we do go, talk about baseball, but don't be showing your pitches, OK?"

"Are you referring to the time I busted apart their lawn ornament with the raw potato?" asked Phil.

"Dear Wife, they asked me about how to throw a split-fingered fastball, it was by request....can I help it if the Garden Fairy statue in the yard was so fragile? Figured it was cast iron...those baby jockeys are cast iron, never would bust one o' them.

"I guess if you want to go, we can go. Can you find a baby

sitter for the little one?"

While Phil was out of the room, Sally called a girl she had heard of who did babysitting.

"Brenda, this is Ms. Daffodil, we live at 326 Pinehurst Drive. Are you available for babysitting this evening?"

"Yes, I do babysitting."

"We have this kind of unusual situation. My husband thinks he's a bird so he wears a big bird suit, and he says 'WHEEEE-CHEEE-CHEEE' sometimes.

"There is no actual kid to baby-sit, just a beach ball my husband thinks is an egg, you see....easy to take care of, you don't have to actually sit on the egg, beach ball, that is. Don't be surprised if he says 'WHEEEE-CHEEE-CHEEE'...just bird talk, ignore it, I do...."

"Ms. Daffodil, you know, I...wait a moment,...it's a text message..Oh my Gosh, my grandmother has died! Can't baby-sit after all, sorry."

"Oh, Brenda, that's awful,...I...."

"I have to go now, Ms. Daffodil, sniff."

After Brenda had hung up, she said, "Mom, do you know the Daffodils? They're a few blocks away on Pinehurst Drive."

"No, Dear, I don't know them."

"I can tell you one thing, they're dillies! Daffy dillies!"

140

Phil returned with his feathers smoothed and topknot combed. "Did you find a babysitter?"

"No, I called one but she couldn't come."

They borrowed a baby carriage from next door and put the beach ball in it and headed to the dinner party.

"Remember, no throwing potatoes. And think of some things to talk about besides childish baseball pranks, like you told about last time."

"That reminds me, I'll demonstrate how to give a hotfoot! Best joke there is! All you need is kitchen matches."

****

The first game Phil pitched as a bird, the other team squawked about the bird suit, but the umps said there was no rule against bird suits as far as they could see. The crowd was happy to have some novelty. If you've ever watched baseball, you know it's pretty boring waiting for something to happen besides players standing around punching their mitts and adjusting their uniforms.

Opposing batters complained that they couldn't see the ball release; it came out of an explosion of wings, bird feet, and feathers, but the umps sided with Phil's team.

In the third inning, Phil waved his catcher out to talk.

"Listen, Stubby, next pitch is gonna be a raw potato, right down the middle, a fat pitch a school kid could hit. Now if he misses or doesn't swing, return it quick so the ump doesn't see it. OK?"

"Phil, the ump will throw you outta the game."

"Wouldn't be the first time, hah!"

They set up and Phil fired it in. Jake, the batter, saw this wobbly brown ball sailing in belt high and his big swing caught it dead center. 'Course it just busted in pieces and he stood there wondering where it went. To confuse the umpire, Phil pretended to catch a line drive, and held up the actual ball. DELETED fans cheered.

Didn't fool the ump 'cause he had potato gobs on his face. He ran out to the mound and made one of those dramatic gestures meaning "You're outta the game, Buddy." The ump was hopping mad and Phil went hopping to the locker room.

Casey came out, though, and said the batter should be out, he had two strikes already, he didn't hit the ball, so it was his third strike. But the ump one-umpped him. The actual ball wasn't thrown so it wasn't in play; it was equivalent to a practice swing.

Attendance was way up for Phil's next game, they wanted to see the bird-man, expecting he would be thrown out before long and it might be the only chance to see a giant bird smoking a stogie and pitching.

"The fans love you, kid," Casey said to his ace pitcher. "You ready?"

"Sure, I feel strong, Boss. Only thing is, I still can't fly,

&^%$#%."

"Listen, next time, you'll fly, with a little help."

At Phil's next game, the fans may have wondered about the long zip line cable going from the left field stands across the mound and up to the bleachers behind home plate.

But not for long. There was a great trumpet fanfare, and the crowd cheered as the six-foot Carter's Grosbeak glided and flapped down to the mound, skidding to a standup landing. He took a bow and unhooked himself from the zip line cable and smoothed his feathers and was ready to go. Almost. The bat-boy ran out with his cigar. He clamped it in his beak while the bat-boy lit it for him. Now he was ready.

There were complaints, but no rules were found against players flying to their positions. The Powers That Be had also neglected to outlaw cigars.

There being no shortage of jokers on Casey's team, soon three of them obtained colorful and feathery bird costumes of their own. Was the dignity of the venerable game being damaged? The roaring fans didn't think so.

The players might have tired of the cumbersome bird costumes, but they discovered something. The wings were stretchy and stored energy as they hauled back to throw, and added a nice snap to their throws. Especially after they sewed bungee cords into them.

Apparently believing in the saw, "The more, the merrier" more players got feathery costumes. Soon the DELETED team had a bird at every position. Other teams complained they were trapping the ball with the huge wings, which was true, but they got away with it.

****

"No, no, you are all in violation, you have no licenses, you have no bodies!" Thaddeus Thistle shouted.

"Wake up! Wake up!" said his wife, Bess, shaking him.

"It was awful," he said, perspiring. "I was trying to get to work, but the road was filled with junk cars, rusty hulks lurching out from every yard blocking the street......they had no drivers!! ....like ghosts!!....."

"Before that, I took a big box of violation notices to mail to residents, but the post office was locked and abandoned, with windows broken, so I set out to deliver them myself, but the grass in all the lawns was so thick I could hardly walk, my feet got tangled and I dropped all the notices...I reached for them...pink plastic flamingos pecked at my hands....ohhhh."

"Have some hot cocoa, Dear, and try rocking back and forth like you do sometimes. It calms you."

The next day Mr. Thistle talked to the therapist he used to go to years ago.

"Dr. Grindle, the dreams I described, endless strange dreams... and this morning they ran out of hazelnut coffee at the shop and I burst into tears. What does it mean, Doc?"

"It means you're a crazy man, Thad," said Dr. Grindle.

144

Mr. Thistle decided to quit his town manager job and become a librarian in DELETED Brook, DELETED.

****

On Tuesday, Phil stayed out late playing poker with some pals. He had a nice advantage: nobody could see his face since he had on the bird outfit. At least his face wouldn't give away his bluffs. He lost anyway. Many beers were consumed.

Late the next morning Phil woke up.

"Man, I got a hangover! I feel like I've been asleep for days. You won't believe the dream I had. I was a bird with feathers and a big beak, Man, ...and with big bird feet...ha,ha,ha!"

He stumbled to the bathroom and splashed water over his bleary-eyed face.

"Sally, I slept a long time. Last thing I remember that ball got me right here, just bounced off my head. Did we lose that game yesterday?"

Sally quickly tossed the bird suit into the closet.

"Gotta get to the park," said Phil, pulling on his street clothes.

"Have some coffee, Phil."

"You're a sweetheart, Sal!" he said as he took some big slurps.

Through the window he saw the carefully woven giant bird's nest. "Whaaa...?" He went outside and came back. "My Gawd, Sally, there's a huge twisted pile of branches up in our trees! Was there a tornado?"

"Look, call Tony, our yard man, to get rid of it, will you? What a mess! Well, I'm off to play ball."

Sally finished her coffee and then took a little walk to the Salvation Army Store. She donated a bird suit and a beach ball.

Phil was at the house when she returned.

"I practiced awhile, but my head aches, I'll lie down a spell. Gotta be back at 2:00 for the game.

"Casey's gone crazy, he has the whole team dressed up as birds. Said where's my bird outfit. Guess he wanted me to dress up, too! I told him, I ain't gonna dress up as a dumb bird!

"I'll be out there pitchin' surrounded by big birds! They don't pay me enough, Sally."

Aunt Beak's Antiques

It's me, Elroy Dentroone. Went from drifter to Deputy Sheriff in one jump, if I may brag. First day on the job I met Fred. A nice enough fella with no discernable function in life. Just sittin' at the coffee shop.

"Why do you carry two guns, Elroy?" he asked.

I explained because Allan Pinkerton, the famous crime fighter, carried two guns.

"But, my Dear Fellow, Allan Pinkerton wore a suit and tie and straw boater and no gun, his lieutenants carried guns," said Mr. Know-It-All.

"Well, maybe it was Wyatt Earp I was thinking of…"

"Nope, only one gun," he said kind of quickly.

"Bat Masterson."

"One gun."

"Johnny Dresden."

"Never heard of 'im."

"How soon they forget." 'Course I just made up the name.

The sheriff had no takers for the job, except me. Real small town, Light Bulb, Arkansas. That's a good idea for a name, don't you think?

Little bitty station house. Also, forgot to tell you, half of my job is town maintenance like fixing potholes. Bummer, there. I suppose you think we had squad cars. Whooie, no, sorry, Bob. Had two motor scooters. What brand? Wimpmobile, I think it was.

On Tuesday I got back from my morning patrol and had a coffee with the boss, Sheriff McCoy. Dill was always reading the crime news. In the Little Rock paper, there was a pic of the **Boxcar Bandit**. Crazy guy who rode freights, stole bicycles on short stops of the train.. He had a yellow outfit. Pinkertons nabbed him, but he jumped bail.

Dill was trying to bring me up to speed on law enforcement. "Here's one," he said. "Bank robber dressed as an old lady. That's the secret: to watch for those old ladies!" I said I would. "Their purses will be heavy 'cause a gun is heavy."

He had a purse and demonstrated. "I'll be the old lady imposter." He walked first with the ordinary purse-load then with the .45 automatic purse-load. Gosh, he was right, it pulled the straps taut. "Also, Elroy, notice how a man walks straight ahead, but an old lady will rock side to side, like a turkey."

On my perimeter cruise, I found a dandy hill to try some modest jumping with the Wimpmobile scooter. Hardly any daylight, nothin' like a Phantom 500 Motocross, of course.

****

On my way back I met Bev. She was indeed a beauty to behold! Cashmere sweater and scarf, light brown hair that tended to fall in her face so she'd sweep it away. She seemed to be smiling even when not smiling. Stephen Foster would have written a song about Bev.

She recently inherited the antique shop right across from the station. Shop was kinda run-down, had a sign with a bird wearing granny glasses. Bev beamed a big smile and showed me around her shop and said to please stop by anytime. I certainly would, I assured her.

This gracious young lady invited me to sit and have a coffee. "Do you believe in ghosts, Mr. Dentroone?" she asked.

"Funny you should ask that...not long ago I was sound asleep and a voice woke me up:"

"Melvin! Give me my gold watch!"

I mumbled, "I'm Elroy."

"&^%^^%$, wrong house!"

I said, "You're kinda scary. Are you a ghost?"

149

"What do you think, Binky?" he says.

"Kinda rude, I'd say. Probably just a spooky dream, but I don't tell everybody about it, because it sounds crazy to be talking to ghosts."

Maybe she was even crazier than me, because she invited me to sit in on a little bridge game with her and her Uncle Ned and Aunt Mabel, who were both, unfortunately, dead. Just two empty chairs, but Bev would talk as though they were right there, and so I did, too.

Being wispy spirits they couldn't actually pick up and play the cards so Bev and I had to do that for them, and though they always accepted offers of coffee, and so on, we had to do the drinking and eating the little cakes.

Bev and Uncle Ned won the hand, and I had to keep going on my duties.

"Elroy, please come by again, Uncle Ned and Aunt Mabel both invited you, too."

"Sure thing," I said.

****

Except for two bicycle thefts, not much police business went on in Light Bulb over the next few days. I kept asking about getting better transportation, maybe Harleys, for example, but Dill said we had only a skimpy budget, y'know. On a more positive note, I found out that law enforcement organizations can get FREE Defense Department surplus. Yup. I looked over the latest listings and sent in my request for two bazookas.

Wednesday evening. It was dark by the time I was walking back to my rooming house. Not many houses along that road and as I went by the abandoned old Walker house, I saw a light up in an upstairs window!

Old Walker died 20 years back and his place was all boarded up. I would go by all the time and it was always dark and spooky, but this time a light. Somebody's in there! Must be some tramps illegally trespassing. I went in silently, on up the stairs, my two guns at the ready.

I said, "Police! Open up!" No answer so I hid behind the door jamb and kicked it open and went on through to catch 'em. I saw four tough-looking characters sitting around a table like they'd been playin' poker. They all had guns pointing at me! The door triggered a flash camera and I could see this was a gag, just cardboard cutouts. Very funny. There was a note on the table: "OK, Deputy, you got us! We give up!" Signed: "The Dalton Gang".

I was a good sport and took the cutouts to the lockup and propped them up in the cell.

'Course I knew it had to be Bev's doing, I hardly knew anybody else in town. Next morning I went to see Bev on my way to the station. "Hey, Bev, I don't want to brag, but I nabbed the Dalton Gang last night. Caught 'em flatfooted, they were armed but I got the drop on 'em."

"Really? That's very impressive, Elroy, you bein' new on the force and all!"

She came over to the station with her camera. The boss wasn't happy, gave me a little lecture about damage to the dignity of law enforcement.

"But Boss, I'm just a victim of this little gag," I said.

Bev took pictures of the four mean-looking hoods in the cell. "Dill, stand over in front of the cell for a minute, will you?"

"No, now quit clowning around and get rid of those. Elroy, you should be working on the bicycle theft case."

Bev said, "Aw, Dill, don't be such a sour pickle!"

****

I was at Bev's the next day when a customer appeared in a yellow suit and tie. Pretty Snazzy. He had an old safety bicycle with a big bulb horn.

"It's an antique, Ms. Trills, 1920 vintage."

"How are you today, Mr. Canary?" Bev introduced me, and explained that Mr. Canary came often with old bikes to sell.

Bev was interested, even though she had a few bikes already. I headed off to complete my appointed rounds.

No leads on the missing bikes. Both disappeared from back-yards on Railroad Street. Boss said we need to work up a criminal profile to home in, narrow it down. "It might be a man dressed as an old lady," he said.

The sheriff was kind of conservative. He wouldn't even go for my idea of using drag racing fuel in the scooters. "Nitro-methane 90%, alky 10%, that'll give 'em some pep!" I said. "I used to be an auto mechanic, y'know, Boss."

Wouldn't buy it. Also, he kind of scoffed when I brought home the two bazookas from the Army Depot at Hamilton.

Still another bicycle went missing in town. Railroad Street. We went to the scene and took plaster casts of all the footprints we could find. "No small shoe sizes," observed Sheriff McCoy, "so can't be a kid, unless they wore big shoes just to fool us."

"Boss, remember that many times the butler is the culprit," I cleverly pointed out.

Dill said, "Hey, right, and there is a butler in town. That fellow Pendelton, at that place with the big lawn, what's his name? Sir Worthington Walsh-Cummings."

'Course I immediately regretted my comment. He sent me out to find out the butler's shoe size and then see if they matched any of our plaster casts. Now how am I gonna do that?

Can't just ask stuff like that, you'd tip off the suspect and he'd be on his guard. I staked out the place. The butler walked to get lunch every day at 12:15 PM to a place in town. I would just make a nice muddy patch for him to walk over and then I'd make a cast of his shoe prints when he was out of sight!

Next day I got to a likely spot for my clever trap at noon (in my civies, so the suspect wouldn't know we were on his trail). Trouble was I had no mud, sidewalk was clean a whistle, so I scooped up some dirt from a nearby garden.

Wouldn't you know it? A little old lady came trotting out and she wasn't very polite about telling me to clear the &^%$%%^ out of there or she'd call the police. I tried to tell her that I <u>was</u> the police, but she seemed to be somewhat deaf and didn't understand my simple plan about the footprints in the dirt, so I decided to leave well enough alone before she hit me with her cane. Pendelton was coming. I'd have to try again another day.

****

I loved visiting Bev but, personally, I wouldn't give a nickel for any of the junk in her shop, except there was a dandy of an antique pistol. Was that for sale? Bev didn't want it, but was reluctant to sell it because it belonged to dear Uncle Ned, and maybe he would feel bad.

Bev put those Dalton Gang cutouts up in the store along with a big print of me with my two guns capturing the cardboard criminals. Even made up postcards of that photo, $1.00. OK, Bev, enough, already!

Thursday. No antique customers at Bev's so we sat down for coffee and bridge. Uncle Ned was a pretty good player but he always bid too high.

I said to Ned, "Say, Ned, what do you think about your old antique Colt .45 there in the case? Think Bev should keep it, or sell it?"

Ned said, "Don't keep it on my account, I can't even lift a playing card."

"OK, then, Ned," Bev said. "I'll ask Aunt Mabel about the

price."

"Aunt Mabel was the one who looked up all the items in the pricing guides like Scalawag's or Sharpie's," she explained. Bev leaned close to Mabel. "What's that, Aunt Mabel? Oh, the stair railing at the front door?"

"Elroy, maybe you can look at that for us. How can it be fixed, I wonder? She worries she might fall."

"Thought ghosts just floated. They don't weigh anything."

Getting back to important things, I said, "Yep, that's a mighty nice pistol, I might want to buy it. When I get some money ahead. Of course, I've gotta be sure to have money to get presents for beautiful young ladies, or to take them out for lavish dining or trap shooting."

"Elroy, you could ask any Light Bulb girl. It would brighten her day!"

****

Time went by. Picture a fan blowing a few pages off a calendar. More bicycles stolen. Pendelton had been writing some comic novels and became richer than his boss and relocated to New York City. We scratched him off the suspect list. Could have henchmen still active, I suppose.

It was a cloudy Tuesday. I saw a "**For Sale**" sign in front of Bev's store!

I went in and talked to Bev. "Yes, I'll have to close Mabel and Ned's shop.....their life's work you see here. Just not enough customers, losing money day by day."

"I'm sorry to hear it, Bev."

It was sad. Or was it? Maybe a few dump runs were called for, really. I wandered amongst the piles of ancient household debris. I spotted a wind-up gadget.

As a rule, I've got no use for antiques but this was a real gem from the 1850's. An old woman on the end of a horizontal wire went around and around trying to catch a pig....but the pig always stayed ahead. It would sometimes slow down, and the woman would be just about to get it, but whoosh, the pig would put on speed and get away again!

"This is fabulous, Bev! Why didn't you tell me you had this?"

"Elroy, the shop is full of hokey flibberty-gibbets like that. I've got three of those. Nobody even looks at it."

Not to be deterred, I took a photo of this gem and sent it to (talk show person) or TSP for short.

And wasn't my skeptical friend Bev surprised when TSP immediately bought the precious antique charmer via mail! Not only that, but talked about it, praised and admired it on TV, as was only to be expected. Bev got many letters requesting more of the wind-up marvels.

Too bad only two more in the shop, and not likely many around and about for the potential buyers. Now, I'm not boasting, but I did have a solution to this, which I outlined over coffee to Bev and Uncle Ned and Aunt Mabel.

"Here's the answer. Just make reproductions! People don't care if it's a copy, they want the substance and it will all be there for them. I know a guy who can get stuff made in Pacific Rim countries- good quality, fast and cheap! It's not your normal antique shop activity, but a buck is a buck, n'est-ce pas?"

Dear Reader, I'm so happy to tell you, it came to pass! A month later Bev hired extra help to handle hundreds of orders a day! Aunt Beak's Antiques became a destination sensation! They came to pick up the old woman and the pig and bought many other antiques (junk) too.

****

"We aren't just hicks in Light Bulb," said the boss. "We got our first break in the bicycle case. As you know, we hid GPS transmitters in many bikes in this and surrounding towns. A few days ago, one was stolen!

"I've been following the locations. Follows the train track route as far as Fargo, then comes back on the same route. Then repeats. Back and forth. It doesn't make any sense. It must be a faulty GPS. What fool would steal a bike and ride it over bumpy railroad ties anyway?"

****

Would you believe, in rummaging around some more in Bev's junk I found another hit from 1850! A Pancake Man bank! Let me explain. A little charming carnival vendor is making pan-cakes. Of course, this is a cast iron toy bank, so the pancakes are coins which you place in the little skillet.

Push on his chef's hat and Pancake Man flips the pancake (coin) into the air and it comes down and goes into the bank or perhaps onto the floor. Most of the time onto the floor, but that just gives you another chance for fun.

I didn't hesitate to send a photo to TSP. Not to brag, but I predicted that TSP would be as struck as I was by this creative marvel from the past. TSP called Bev and gushed, I'm told, about Pancake Man and arranged to broadcast a whole show from Aunt Beak's Antiques!

Bev said, "Why not?"

Bev hired four of the local folks to help in the store. It was busy from dawn 'til dark.

We still got a bridge game in most mornings, though, in fact, the boss complained I was taking too many coffee breaks. Bev had to ask Aunt Mabel all the time about prices. She probably wished she could rest in peace.

"Do you think the shopping carts and checkout lines have changed the character of our little antique shop?" asked Bev.

****

I was having a beer with Barney Grubb and he was tellin' about the cussed ole Buick he had, gonna have to junk it.

One thing and another, we thought it would make a dandy target for bazooka practice. The town gravel pit is the perfect place 'cause you have the huge sand pit backdrop to shoot toward. We towed that wreck out and I let Barney have first shot. The fool missed high and outside, just exploded sand all over. Next was my turn and it was a hit.

Must have been quite a bit of gas in the tank 'cause the flaming debris went far enough to hit the town truck, and caught it afire and caused another gas tank explosion which was a serious KABOOM! I can tell you. We ducked down flat and nobody was hurt. About then I figured maybe it was time for me to be drifting again.

****

I made a rushed dash in to say goodbye to Bev.

"Bev, I'd love to stick around with you and I could always show up here again, but remember, I'm a shiftless ne'er-do-well."

I gave her a big hug and was out the door. She blew me a kiss and I was off running for the tracks.

I was lucky enough to catch a freight before long and it was an express. It stopped at Kelton and I got off. To my surprise there was Mr. Canary, just hopped out of the boxcar ahead of mine.

"Howdy," I called, and we talked.

"I take a trip now and then, to see my Aunt Tweety, here in town. Going first class is nice but I like the boxcar rates."

I had to agree with him on that.

"This was my last trip, as a matter of fact. I've decided to

159

retire. Good luck to you, Young Man!" With that he got on his bike and rode off to visit Aunt Tweety.

Improv Novel

"Listen Sam, look at this book, <u>How to Write an Improv Novel</u>. It really makes sense....you pretend you are the characters and act out the story... it flows like water! We have this tape recorder to capture everything. Let's give it a try..... we'll write a novel of the sea, for example!"

Joe: "Listen, we'll run down to my uncle's costume shop....it's closed, of course, but I've got a key, 'cause I help him there sometimes. He won't mind if we just borrow a few period clothes."

An hour later, the two friends are back in their fourth-floor walk-up and after they open a couple of beers, the literary experiment begins:

Sam is dressed like a banker's son who has wandered onto the gangplank and up to the ship's deck.

Sam: "I'll start it off. I'm a greenhorn, see, I want to go to sea,

Reginald Danderspoon. You be the person on the ship."

Joe: "Ok, I'll be…wait, wait, Reginald Danderspoon? ….we're not doing a comedy here, Sam…."

Sam: "Well, I don't care, the name doesn't matter. OK, Reggie Sandsprinkle, then."

Joe: "What? I don't think anybody was ever, ever, named…"

Sam: "OK, let's not get hung up on a silly thing, Reggie… I know, Reggie Blank… Blank means we'll fill it in later."

Joe wears a rough cotton shirt and flaxen vest, red neck scarf and headband and scuffed brown shoes with buckles.

Joe: "I'll be the sailor on the ship. Bosun's Mate, Goose Benderbeak."

Sam: "Goose Benderbeak?…are you just trying to get back at me, or something?"

Joe: "No, no, I thought it'd be good. We should have some flavor to the names, just not like Danderspoon…well, look, make it Goose Blank. Let's get on with the good parts. Like the book said, the dialog is paramount, we get right into the characters, and the book writes itself!"

Sam: "All right, we're off…Reggie goes up the gangplank, …tromp, tromp, carrying a sack with his stuff…"

Sam (Reggie B.): "Hi, Friend, I want to sign aboard…."

Joe (Goose B.): "Whar you gooin' Pansy?.. Gat otter har!"

Sam: "Hold it, 'goon pansy'? That's an odd name to call me...."

Joe: "No, no, not 'goon' I said 'gooin', it's British dialect for 'going'."

Sam: "Oh, OK, I'll keep going...now I'm Reggie B.: 'Sir, I wish to speak to the captain.'."

Joe (Goose B.): "Git yer skinny bones dan back the plank, or I'll bust ya wid me marlinspike!"

Sam: "Wait, we're not getting anywhere...."

Joe (Goose B.): "I tole ya' ...."

Sam: "No, I'm me now, not Reggie. We are stuck ... How am I going to get the job if you keep kicking me off the ship?"

Joe: "Well, it's realistic, you go, in 1850, try to get a &^^$% job on a ship...., see, we gotta establish these are rough sea-dogs, y'know."

Sam: "All I'm sayin' ...how the &%$%^% is Reggie gonna get on the &^%%$ ship??"

Joe: "OK, OK, let's keep going. The captain comes along, now. Goose says, 'Skipper, I was jest about t'throw this runt over the side....' wait, we need a captain here."

Sam: "Hold on, Joe. Why does Goose say 'We need a captain here.'? He's already there."

Joe: "No, no, I said that part! We need a player to play the part."

Sam: "I'll be the captain."

Joe: "How can you be the captain? You'd be talking to yourself!"

Sam: "Hold one moment. I'll see if Silvia's home."

Unfortunately, Silvia is good-looking, has lots of admirers and doesn't wish to associate with her nerdish neighbors, Sam and Joe, and barely tolerates them. She doesn't answer the phone because she has caller ID.

Sam: "No answer, let's just stop by and knock. We have to keep our momentum, Joe."

"Knock, knock." Silvia sees who it is by looking through the peephole.

"Sam, I don't have time to talk now, I'm sorry your girlfriend left you. It's because you're a dork."

Sam: "It's not about my girlfriend this time. Joe's with me."

Silvia: "Dork I and Dork II. Did you lose your busboy jobs already?"

Joe: "See, we're writing a novel…it's a sea epic…"

Silvia: "I can't read your &^%$% novel. There are 10 million people in New York who could have been my neighbors. Why did I get you?"

Joe: "It's to help with the novel…it won't take long."

Silvia opened the door.

Sam: "Thanks, Silvia, I thought you weren't going to let us in."

Silvia: "I wasn't, but I just remembered my computer's locked up, maybe you can take a look at it…"

Sam: "Listen, this won't take long…we're doing a very important bit of play-acting, and it's a new method, a proven method."

Sam and Joe explained the characters and where their historical action thriller novel had progressed to so far.

Silvia: "OK, OK, as long as I get my computer fixed… I'll be Captain Monica Roundstern."

Joe: "Pretend you're a man for this part, OK?"

Silvia: "Why can't it be a woman captain, Mr. Chauvinist?"

Joe: "Not historically accurate."

Silvia: "I'm not doing it unless it's a woman."

Sam: "OK, OK, Silvia, let's just keep going. See, you, as the skipper, come walking along the deck. Then I get to speak to you. But first, we have here a costume. See if this coat will fit."

Silvia is quickly at home with the brass-buttoned coat and

tricorn hat, which she wears with aplomb. "I need a sash and sword, you know," she said. But they decided to plunge ahead without those particulars.

Sam (Reggie B.): "Captain Roundstern, I'm Reggie Blank, and I'm looking to sign aboard your ship."

Silvia (Captain R.): "You're a mite skinny and too young, too, Boy, better grow up some before ya think to sail the High Seas!"

Sam (Reggie B.): "But Sir,...."

Silvia (Captain R.): "Don't call me Sir, you puppy!"

Sam (Reggie B.): "Ma'am, I'm sorry, wait, we don't want that part.."

Silvia (Captain R.): "Don't want what part, Laddie? Air you daft?"

Sam: "No, no, I'm me now. It was my mistake, called you 'Sir', just leave that out, OK? Here, I'll start again."

Sam (Reggie B.): "But Ma'am, I have a letter of introduction from Sir Manfred Cupcake."

Silvia (Captain R.): "Why didn't you say so? We were secret lovers you know, just last year. He called me Gumdrop and I called him Cupcake."

Joe: "Wait, wouldn't you keep that quiet?"

Silvia (Captain R.): "Reggie, Matey, don't mention it around the ship, OK? It just slipped out!"

Joe: "No, I'm me now, I mean it's …the Captain wouldn't just blab stuff like that."

Silvia: "Oh, let's keep going."

Silvia (Captain R.): "Young man, climb to the crow's nest, and bring back the spyglass before this minute-glass runs out and you've got the job!"

"Knock, knock." Silvia let in her friend, Lizzy.

Silvia: "Hey, Lizzy, come join us, this is fun. You know my nerdy neighbors, right? Listen, we need you to play a part… it's a new way to write a novel!"

Silvia quickly filled in the details of the novel's progress, and Liz was game to participate.

Silvia: "Lizzy, you play the part of the wife of Sir Manfred Cupcake, OK, a fine lady. Dignified and a power figure in London Society."

Liz: "Sure, I get it. By speaking the parts, the thing takes on a life that just writing on paper can't."

Silvia puts her hand on Sam's shoulder.

Silvia (Captain R.): "You've got the job, Pip! I'll call you 'Pip', methinks! Stow yer gear and make haste. I want you to go ashore to the livery and get us a cabriolet. I must attend a small function before we sail for the South Seas!"

Silvia outlines the next part. Small social gathering that evening, but: Lady Cupcake has suspicions about last year's indiscretion regarding Sir Cupcake and the Captain!

Silvia (Captain R.): "Pip, you watch the carriage while I'm at the dinner party, there's a good lad."

Silvia described the next scene: the elegant dining room, gleaming silver, a sumptuous table.

Liz (Lady C.): "Why, it's Captain Roundstern, how nice to meet you. Have you by any chance met Sir Cupcake? I suppose not, even though you both belong to the Royal Yacht Club and he goes there all the time. Especially when the fleet is in port."

Silvia (Captain R.): "How do you do? You must be Sir Cupcake's mother, then. No, you're his wife? Oh, forgive me, the candle light is rather dim. Why, it's a pleasure to meet you both for the very first time ever, Lady and Sir Cupcake."

Liz (Lady C.): "So nice of you to drop by before you set sail. I hope you have had time to put your affair, I mean your affairs in order before you go to sea. I do hope you don't sail off the edge of the world and plunge into the abyss to your death!"

Silvia now said they really needed to go into high gear, and they needed a man to be Sir Cupcake, and they all headed for a small café where she knew the bartender, Jake, who had a British accent and would be perfect for the part. Jake wasn't that busy at the bar, so he said, "Sure."

Jake (Sir C.): "Captain, will you have some Chablis?"

Liz (Lady C.): "I'm afraid it is not as strong as the large mugs of 90 proof grog you serve on your ship at evening meals and at noon and at tea time and at breakfast and at midnight."

Silvia (Captain R.): "Lady Cupcake, What savory lobster, but of course there are claws. I'll beware of sharp claws tonight."

Liz (Lady C.): "You're very brave to sail the high seas; a lonely job, I suppose. But of course there are 50 men to keep you company."

Silvia (Captain R.): "Lady C.! One of the lobster claws fell off your plate... oh, that's your hand, sorry, heh, heh."

Jake (Sir C.): "I always like a dash of salt on mine. Captain, would you care for some salt?"

Liz (Lady C.): "She's an Old Salt, herself, Dear, ha, ha. Of course I don't mean old, as in wrinkled old. I don't mean you have ugly crow's feet by your eyes, I mean old as in experienced. Experienced with sailors,...uh, I mean,... sailing."

It just happened that Liz had some good ideas involving three beautiful sisters, favorites at the court of Queen Victoria and Prince Albert, and the dashing young Crimean War hero, Henry Cartier and some other characters. They had no trouble en-listing the help of several tipsy bar patrons to speak these colorful parts.

Hours later:

Sam: "But, Silvia, Liz, where do we get back to the whaling ship and my character, young Reggie? This was going to be a seafaring novel, you know."

Silvia: "That'll be the perfect ending, Sam. Reggie returns two years later and the palace intrigue and the three love triangles will be resolved. That would wrap things up. No room for more Reggie character, it'll be too long, it's War and Peace length already!"

Sam: "But, Silvia, we never even put out to sea."

Silvia: "Hey! Gather 'round everybody, let's play back the tape. I want to hear this! We'll just transcribe it and we've got a winner! Play it, Sam!"

Sam: "Well, OK. I'll rewind and...."

There is a long pause. Silvia, Lizzy, Joe, Jake, Erma, Nate, Bullnose, Muffin, and a yellow dog lean closer to observe Sam fumbling with the tape player.

Sam: "I...I forgot to start the tape. We didn't record anything........ Gosh, look at the time. I'd better, be going.... Hey, this has been fun, y'know."

Silvia, Lizzy, Joe, Erma, Nate, Bullnose, Muffin, and a yellow dog: "WHAAAAAAAAAAAAAT??????"

Roadside Days

Now you, as a reader, might ask as follows:

"How did you, Sherm, not usually a gullible patsy, get roped into working at The Two Pigs Wonder Cave, a so-called roadside attraction?"

Good question. It's because I made a big mistake. I let sister Nell buy me two tires for the old Chevy I had and why did I ever do that because now it's like she saved my life and not bought two 15x20 Royals, used but pretty new.

Well, I had two flats at the same time and no work going on at the garage, and I was in the hole from the Vegas trip with Wheezy so I was desperate to a degree. Not so long after, she cried and whined for help, so, not to be a heel, I had to.

'Course it had to be just when I'd racked up over 11,000 points on the Space Girls pinball at Happy's Garage, even though the left flipper's got no rubber left at all either. If you've ever played Space Girls you'd know the left flipper is the most important for success.

"You know I wouldn't ask you to help if it wasn't important, Shermy." She calls me Shermy when she wants something.

"The Perpetual Stream has just stopped. First it got less and less like I told you before, but now not a drop. I don't know why."

"Well," I says, "I can't imagine that rusty old pump would stop working after only 100 years."

"Shermy, we have to get it going……..it's been flowing the beautiful clear flow and what would our patrons think if it stops? Our sign says, in big letters, after all……'Perpetual Stream'……'Never stopped since 1880, etc……' 'even in droughts, keeps going!'."

I wrote 345-675-7869 on a card and gave it to her.

"What's that?"

"Plumber in Westville, cheap and worth every cent."

"Sheeeermaaaan!" she says, whispering pretty loud. "Now you know we can't let a stranger see the secret of the Perpetual Stream!"

So of course nothing would do but I have to drop everything to schlep my toolbox to the cave. Some oil and a few raps with a hammer and the Perpetual Stream was going again. Of course old Ned the tramp showed up at Happy's and used up all my Space Girl free games.

****

My reward for the above good deed was to get manipulated into doing the Tour Talk. Gawd, I hate the boring Tour Talk. Starts with Elbert Garrett finding the cave back in 1880. He was, how interesting!, a farmer. Digs some limestone from a side hill for his foundation. What's this? A hole! Digs a little. A cave!

When I did the spiel, I stretched things a bit, made Elbert a Jesse James pal escaping and hiding in this fortuitous cave, but nevertheless being finally discovered and killed in the ensuing gun battle. At this point in the narrative, I'd show the marks in the rock made by .45 caliber bullets, which in truth I made with a No. 2 ball peen hammer. Nell found out and objected to putting her family in a bad light.

"Your great grand-pappy is not going to come back from the grave and object to a little slander, Nell," I said.

Sure, it's OK for Nell to put in the imaginary Theodore Roosevelt visit with his phony guest book signature. It's OK to tell her fictitious tale of Pappy finding all the Indian arrow-heads. Pappy made up all these wax arrowheads and put 'em in a glass case, still there from when he started this cave scam in '34 or so. You'd a thought those Indians had an arrowhead factory right here. Pappy inherited a farm of cliffs and rocks but it had a cave. A short, boring cave. He imported bats, but they left.

I was right here when she and her drifty friend Irma dreamed up the Incredible Tiny People exhibit out of thin air! "Listen, Honey, my boy, Booney, found these squirrel bones in the woods. Or maybe it's a weasel. But some of them look like little bitty HUMAN bones! Does that give you an idea?"

So they made this COMPLETELY BOGUS exhibit about how these bones were found in this very cave, and were authenticated as genuine tiny early hominid bones-ONE FOOT TALL HUMANS!! An evolutionary branch that had died out thousands of years ago! Photo of Dr. Dennis Crampton, Nobel Prize in Archeology winner (Irma's uncle Fred smoking a pipe), declaring "Definitely genuine!", etc. After all, there were once tiny horses, right? Pictures of eohippus bones.

The thing is, when you are a tour guide, after you point out the two round rocks that vaguely resemble loaves of bread or pigs with no legs, tails, or ears, you don't know what to say next, unless you have the benefit of lots of phony history from our Tour Talk. There are two pretty good snouts, but unfortunately one pig has both of them and the other little piggy has none. Like I said, after you describe these wonders, you have pretty much run the table at the old cave.

Kids sometimes ask about the Incredible Tiny People.

"Hey, Dad, who is that scientist, Dr. Crampton?"

Of course Dad never heard of him, but Dad, says, "Oh yes, he's a Nobel Prize winner."

Because he read the phony signs Irma wrote.

"They were pretty advanced, see those tiny arrowheads and the model of the crossbow?"

"Wow, Dad, a crossbow!"

174

Of course sometimes you are going along good in your spiel and you get an 8-year-old heckler:

"There must be some mistake! Those are weasel bones!"

How do you politely tell a kid to shut up their yap and respect their elders who OWN the %$#&$% cave?

Don't get the idea that I have anything really to do with Two Pigs Cave; I just sometimes help. The cave business (scam) is all sister Nell's. I guess it's half owned by her less-than-ambitious excuse for a husband, Pendergast.

Unless it's against the law for an idiot to own land in the state of DELETED. Why did Nell ever marry Pendergast? He ain't handsome. He ain't rich. He ain't smart. He does have a fast car. Old, but fast. He works sometimes picking apples and things but mostly not.

Nell's cave doesn't just dead-end, but has several small tunnels going off in different directions, too small to crawl through, even if you were stupid enough to try. Sometimes there are little noises from the little branch tunnels so naturally I told Nell it was probably Indian ghosts looking for scalps. Now if she has to go there at night she weedles me to go too, not realizing I would run faster than she would outta there.

****

Nell found this book about making flint arrowheads, so one day I'm behind the curtain at the cave chipping. It's real easy to hit your knuckles instead of the flint. My advice is, if you're looking for fake arrowheads, buy authentic ones from a catalog.

A commotion at the front desk.

"Ms. Penny! I hear one now."

A fellow in tan blazer and red bow tie comes rushing through the back area, going for the black hole just behind where I'm sitting with my secret hidden (until now) arrowhead operation.

"Hear that Chi! Chi! Naa-Chi! Sound? Brown-Knuckle bats!"

I say, "Sir, visitors are not allowed in this area....."

Nell comes too, and explains he's Prof. Swindelingerham or somebody, and it's OK, he's looking for rare species and so on. Wants to trap them and study them. Guy climbs into where I would never go, takes pictures and we pull on his legs to get him back out. He's frazzled, lost his glasses and camera in some crevice and he's got bat droppings all over his clothes, but all excited. "I saw them! Definitely Brown-Knuckles!"

Personally, I'm not so excited and would just as soon have politely told him to collect bat droppings elsewhere, but of course Nell gives Prof. S. carte blanche just 'cause he has a suit coat and tie, probably.

Nell's all full of another of her schemes: We'll have this rare bat in a cage out front in the lobby. The big famous Valhalla cave has no rare Brown-Knuckle bat! So nothing would do but Mr. Fancy Pants returns and sets traps and acts like he owns the place. Apparently Nell thinks her mechanical wizard of a brother (me, I modestly mean) can't rig up a trap to catch a stupid bat. Dear Reader, do I sound jealous of Twinkletoes?

How could I be jealous of somebody who wears a bow tie?

The Ivy League bat traps are set. First night, nothing, Second night, nothing. Third night he caught a big rat. Did I laugh up my sleeve? Maybe a tiny hee-hee. Fourth Night: Yes, finally the Devine Prof. S. caught a bat.

Which was duly fawned upon and provided with a luxurious cage. Unfortunately, bats make lousy pets, since they like to sleep all day and catch insects at night in the dark. Another glitch: it wasn't a rare Brown-Knuckle after all, but a garden variety bat, nothing much to brag about, really. Nell, however, doesn't like to admit defeat.

"Shermy, will you try to get Fluffy to eat these crickets? I've got to wait on the visitors."

I toss some choice crickets into the darkroom-cage, but Fluffy just bares his fangs and flutters his taloned wings.

Nell: "It looks pretty strange to me. Bigger than a normal bat. Shermy, go down to the library and get books about bats; let's identify what we've got. Maybe it's not so ordinary. Look for giant bats. Ask the librarian, she's an old bat herself!"

****

I pulled the old Chevy into the library lot, and stepped inside the cool brick building. I could hear the tick-tock of a wall clock. But only a few ticks before: "MR. ULSTER, MAY I SPEAK WITH YOU?" It was Ms. Minocchio.

Yes, she may. She explained authoritatively that the library would appreciate it if I would return <u>Sixgun Justice</u>, <u>Fuel</u>

Injector Manual and Singles' Bar Success and some Batman comics which had run up $9.50 in fines and counting. I said I would. I found an encyclopedia bat article; it had no large ones, no giant bats. Then I pulled out Extinct Species and there was a pretty big bat in there. I promised to round up those other books and escaped with my prize.

Got back to the cave. Nell says, excitedly, "You know, Fluffy looks a lot like this one, 'Giant Bat, narratiosa fangulisanea, believed extinct since 1820'."

However, I have to point out: "But the picture shows those red ears, Fluffy's ears are just gray, don't you see? And the claws ain't the same, either."

"Oh, pooh, pooh, Shermy! Here, you hold the bat, I'll make sure his ears are red enough!" Nell has some nail polish at the ready.

Land o' Goshen, I hate to complain, but Nell gets to be too much sometimes. I said I'd hold the darned little rat, but only if I had gloves so's I'd not get rabies, or turn into a vampire if he scratched. No gloves anywhere, 'til Nell fussed around and found a baseball glove in the lost and found bin.

"Nell! This is a child's baseball glove! My hand hardly fits."

"Don't be such a big baby, Sherm. It's a perfectly good glove, an Andy Waxhandle signature, too."

"Who ever heard of Andy Waxhandle, for cripe's sake?"

I'm trying to imagine Andy Waxhandle, on the farm team for the DELETED Puddle Ducks, .209 lifetime average, sitting on the bench. Just struck out for the third time. Benny the bat-boy says, "Hey Andy, I hear you got an endorsement contract!"

"Yeah, a glove." Goes to get a drink of water.

"Good going, Andy! What company? Rawlings?"

"Naw. Wasn't Rawlings. Hand me that bat there, will you, I got to get ready to hit."

Helpful teammate Hank pipes up, "Tinker-Tot Toy Company, wasn't it, Andy?"

Well, I'll tell you, Fluffy did attack me with his fangs, but the Waxhandle glove protected me sure enough and I was glad to have it and shame on me for joking a little. Fluffy wasn't pleased to get his ears painted, you could see that plain enough, but he did look more like the picture then.

So Nell had a rare bat attraction (scam) after all, and set about to make it front and center in the lobby.

Nebuline from the beauty parlor comes by sometimes to talk to Nell and pretends to be interested in the cave and all, but really just snoops because that's her principal goal in life. Wears many bracelets and beads and accoutrements I don't know the name of and is middle aged, I guess. I think the extra-strength wrinkle cream isn't working for Nebuline.

Of course she sees the new cage and has to snoop. She peeks under the black curtain at Fluffy in his cage. "Rare bat, you say. Yikes, look at those fangs! Look how bright red his ears are."

"That's funny, look. Same shade as my nail polish, 'Scarlet Blush'."

"Nebuline, don't be waking up Fluffy, he sleeps in the day," says Nell, as she quickly closes up the black curtain. Hah!

****

At the garage a few days later I was on my lunch break, doing a little composing of jazz tunes on a little keyboard I have. The boss is busy hammering a headlight into a Dodge.

Phone rings and guess who it was. You're right, it was my sister Nell.

"Sherm, I had Noodle make some signs for the cave. Can you stop by and pick 'em up for me?"

Who is Noodle? I should mention that not so long ago a certain Ms. Noodle Zima bought the modest house on Gulley Road and established a sort of business of painting signs and designing jewelry and such. A woman of really striking beauty, and that kind of open expression that says "What a delightful world, tell me more". Not a few gentlemen around town took notice of the newcomer, and I was one of them, though she's got to be a dozen years my senior. Smiling eyes, bluer than blue.

So that afternoon I went to the house on Gulley Road painted with horizontal pink stripes. It had a sign with a rather decorative typeface saying: "Zima's Emporium". Noodle Zima likes to offer some coffee when you come to her place, which is usually to get a sign painted. "Of course," I said to the

180

coffee offer. "Sounds good, thanks." Oops, she caught me gawking at her. Any man would, she could have stepped right out of "September Morn" by Maxfield Parrish.

She made this giant spider attached to her house, with its hairy legs trying to get into one of her ground-floor windows. Some people think that is creepy. I imagine it's an advertisement: "Within this house is a person who can make giant spiders, should you require one." Noodle likes to talk, which I can ignore pretty well and just enjoy the strong coffee. "Mr. U.," she says, calling me Mr. U., (I don't know why), "I've slept well, as a rule, but I had a dream last night about insects that I didn't like one bit. Big insects. Woke up screaming."

"Not spiders, I hope," says I. "I recommend Interpretation of Dreams, by Dr. F. He gets into that pretty deep, you know, like dreams can be a sign of inner conflicts maybe."

"Speaking of signs," I continued, "Nell wanted that bat sign?"

Noodle had it done. It said: "Please Do Not Feed The Bee".

"Nice work, Noodle, but Nell has a bat not to feed. A big one, you should see it."

"Oh, I'm sorry, you know, I lost the note and just went from memory. I'll fix it up. This can be a 'While You Wait' if you're not in a hurry."

Then she said, "Maybe I put 'Bee' because I have a little bee project going."

I listened with half an ear. Some would just say please shut up and paint the sign, if you don't mind, but Heck, it's free coffee plus Spritz cookies, did I mention that?

"Listen, Mr. U. I know you have great mechanical facility. I believe you fixed Nicky's car which some call a jalopy. Is jalopy a brand that folded like Packard or Reo or what?"

Not waiting for an answer, she continued, "Have you ever wondered if a honeybee would land on a dress like I have on with the colorful flowers and think they were real? In fact I have experimented with that and I found the real requirement is the nectar, or just sugar water is all you need. Interesting, don't you think?"

What do you answer to that? Like Silent Cal, I've found if you say nothing, most any talker runs out of steam after awhile.

"If only we could be in close touch with the beautiful natural world, Mr. U."

Her eyes ranged skyward.

"Flowers printed on fabric is an attempt to do that, but why not do more? Go to my garden, Mr. U. There are flowers, yes, but more: butterflies, moths, bees and wasps. Nature's bounty!"

Noodle rummaged in her sewing basket.

"But think. How can we bring this beauty with us wherever we may go? I will show you. See these artificial honeybees? We can simply attach some of these judiciously by invisible thread to the flowery dress fabric. Nature in all its three dimensional glory!"

"They look real," I said.

"I made them. But it takes too long. What we need is a little assembly line, that I'm sure you can make with all your skill. We need to turn these out by the thousands. You can do that, can't you?"

"No," I said.

****

Nell was pleased with the signs and all was well for a few days, then I got a call.

"Sherm, what'll we do? Fluffy's not eating his crickets! Come and help, we have to take him to the vet's."

Hours later we're at Mel's Small Animal Hospital, two towns over, which means DELETED, 88 miles even though we took the new Route 54 extension. In we go with the black canvas-covered cage with Fluffy and sit down. Some other folks are there waiting.

Nell talks to the lady at the window, "We've got this sick bat, a special rare bat, etc...."

Two kids are running around the place, Future Delinquents of America candidates, and one comes over and wants to peek in the cage and opens it. Fluffy, suddenly not so sick, takes off like a bat out of Hell. A lady was next to us holding her sick tabby cat. Aforesaid sick cat leaped six feet straight up and nailed Fluffy. A direct hit by a furry surface-to-air missile. Result: one dead bat.

"Never mind," says Nell to the lady at the window. We wasted no time getting out of there, carrying the remains of poor Fluffy in a box.

"Look, it's bad luck, but we're not dead yet," says Nell.

"Tell that to Fluffy," I said.

"What I mean is...we can get a taxidermist...and Fluffy can still be a rare bat exhibit, just dead, is all. Do you know anything about taxidermy, Shermy?"

"Nell, you're on your own. I ain't stuffing Fluffy!"

"Well, how about fluffing Stuffy?"

"Hee, hee, hee, hee, hee!"

That was Nell laughing, not me.

****

Next day the phone rings at the garage. It's Nell.

"Listen," she says, excitedly, "an interesting guy stopped in today, he lost his job at a traveling carnival, so he's looking for work. 'Course we don't have any job openings, we got Stringy, the Tour Guide and don't need anybody else. But in talking to Morty, seems he happens to have this two-headed chicken! Can you believe it? See, he's been working for the Happy Time Carnival, but carnies have fallen on hard times since TV came in, so in lieu of salary, they gave him some stuff, since they're bankrupt, and one thing is Betsy-Ellen, one head is Betsy, the other Ellen, left-right sequence, I think.

"What with being temporarily out of work, he's got no place to keep Betsy-Ellen, you see, so he asked could she (they) stay with us here at the cave for a temporary while, so I says sure, that's something our patrons would enjoy seeing. And, Sherm, get this: this (these) chickens are trained to play a game of tick-tack-toe! Morty's got the game board and everything, but didn't bring that yet but he will.

"She's in Fluffy's cage for now, but Morty's got a whole kiosk he can bring if we want. Hear that 'puck-puck'...guess who? Gotta go...customers."

"You sure it's not two chickens in a feathery costume? How many feet they got?"

"Sherm! It's real! Two heads!"

Well, I was glad for Nell. And I guess at least chickens don't have fangs.

****

Happy says, "I started the Colonel's Ford while you was gone, sounds rough as a cement mixer."

"Well, it's got only three plugs is why," I said. "I looked all around for that plug. Maybe landed down in the grease pit."

"We gotta find it."

"You know I can't go down there, Happy, there's snakes."

"There ain't no snakes down there. I go down there all the time."

185

"Maybe you were just lucky each time."

Boss is scowling. "Take a flashlight, you'll see no snakes."

" 'Course not. They'll hide from the light. Then get me!"

"Oh all right, I'll go down and find the %$#&% spark plug!" he says finally.

Happy tromped down and I looked over the edge. A three-foot rattlesnake sprang out and hit his leg!

"What the &^%^*& !!!" he says. Haw! It was a rubber spring snake I put there. From Roy's Joke Shop. Just pull the string when you're ready! Works best in a dark place. Plenty dark in that pit.

"They told me not to hire you, why'd I do it?"

He's always grumbling, ain't he?

"Happy, now don't tell Nell. I ain't pulled it on her yet."

****

Pendergast pulls in with his oversized engine car with illegal noisemakers instead of mufflers.

"Wow, I worked for Haine's farm. I can't pick no more apples, I picked my last apple, Boys. I ordered a turbocharger from Jenkins mail-order. Happy, you gonna let me use your hoist if I need it?"

186

"Gonna Sawsall that body off, Pendy? Turbo won't fit under that hood."

"Naw, Happy, it'll fit."

Two weeks later it comes. Doesn't fit. Pendy cuts a big jagged hole in the hood, and the fender, installs the turbo.

One day later, police pull him over, can't have dangerous jagged body metal. Warning, next time: $200 fine! Pendy pop-rivets on an upside-down five gallon can over everything. Just temporary, he says. He drives around, looks like a big paint can sitting on the hood. Why don't that paint can fall off, anyway?

Happy has never met Noodle. Just seen her around town. He asked in the past, "Would she make a good wife, do you think?"

"If you married Noodle, you might have to change your name to something else, Puzzled, Worried, something like that."

He looked puzzled and worried right then, and continued sandblasting some plugs.

****

Slow day at the garage.

Noodle Zima drives up.

"Hallo! I bought a Jeep, I hope it's not a mistake. From a relative, can a person trust their own kin?"

"I need six quarts of 10W-40 oil."

Happy gets it for her.

"Don't believe we've met," says Happy, looking her over. She's wearing kind of a flowing light azure island dress, a gardenia in her light brown hair. She's maybe 10 years older than me. "They call me 'Happy'. Owner."

"Noodle Zima. If you need any signs, or artwork, stop by. Gulley Road, big white house with a spider."

Arturo came by, had this cheap hunting knife with handle loose. "Durned handle, got any glue, you guys?"

Happy grumbles, but he Superglues it for him.

Said he traded for it, campers were in the woods and he had matches and they didn't so he gave 'em a few and some sticks of firewood.

"OK, watch this," he says and flings the knife at the big maple tree in the yard. Doesn't stick. Hard to get the spin right. Carnies can do it cause they are raised from the cradle throwing knives, probably little baby knifes when they are tykes. Happy and I sit around. Ten throws, never sticks.

Noodle takes the knife from Arturo, flings it, sticks perfectly in the tree with a little twang!

"Circus background?" I have to ask.

"Naw. Nichrome Mountain School of Fine Arts. Performance Art 202. Got an apple?" Happy did, in his lunch box.

"Stand back just a bit."

She threw it straight up about ten feet and with a lunge split that Granny Smith in midair with Arturo's knife. Two halves lay on the ground.

"Just wash 'em, they're OK."

****

Couple days later Happy says, "You know, we've got no good 'Firewood' sign."

"But there's that sign that says $80/face cord. Pretty much tells the deal."

"We do need a more professional sign," Happy continues. "I'll see if I can find somebody that can make one for not too much."

"Try Arnold's Sign Painting."

"That's kind of far away."

"Arturo's brother paints signs, I know."

"But do we know the quality?"

I says, "How about Noodle? She paints signs."

Happy says, "Oh, good idea, I didn't think of her."

"I'll get the phone book, Boss," I says.

I pull it out and turn to the Z's. "That's funny, somebody circled her number already!"

****

I'm at the cave, keeping cool. It's August, and one thing about underground, it's cool. Mailing out "Subterranean Wonderland" flyers.

A few customers (rubes) arrive, yet to be disappointed. Lindy is doing the Tour Talk. Summer help. Studying some aspect of biology. Nice voice, but too quiet, tails off. Suspects our authenticity is not up to Smithsonian standards.

I heard her say, "That signature of Theodore Roosevelt looks kind of wobbly." Nell shrugs, "I believe it was authenticated by my dad." Of course, knowing that she signed it herself.

Hedda Hopper, otherwise known as Nebuline appears, with a guessing game:

"Who has a beat-up GMC black pickup?" She holds up four fingers. "What am I holding up, anyone?"

"I'll tell you, it's the number of times that truck has been at the spider house since the Fourth of July. People might gossip about that kind of thing, you know? It's a mystery to me."

Of course she knows it's Happy's truck, probably knows the engine number, too, in case there are two black, beatup GMCs and she needs to ID them.

****

It's Wednesday. Happy is staying late, working on that crooked muffler for Marcie's Toyota. Happy never works late, so naturally I know something's up. I leave and wait. Then sneak back and peek in the window. Hah! No muffler work, he's got some little machine I never saw before, something like a drill press.

Next day, no sign of any new machine. Arturo is hanging around, so when Happy goes for a greaseburger at Dilly's, I'm busting to tell somebody about this mystery, and he takes the bait and immediately snoops around. Remember, Arturo was the one that started to look, I just… it was his idea.

Hah! Under some rags on the cluttered back room bench: "Easy-Shot Fish Lure Molder", "Molds plastic fly-fishing lures in seconds!"

"Happy never goes fishing, Arturo. What's he up to?" We carefully hide it again when we hear Happy rolling back in.

I knew I could count on Arturo. On Thursday, he comes by carrying a fly fishing rod and reel! "Hey Sherm," he says to me, "I borrowed this rod and reel, but I never fished, what kind of lures can I get for it? You know fishing stuff, don't you?"

Happy blinks and pretends he's not even listening, studying that list of gaskets he's holding.

"Worms, Arturo, big ones, that's good bait," I say.

"Naw, I know you can use worms for sunfish. I'm after them big trout. They take only those bugs on the water, don't they?

Where can I get bug lures, anyway?"

"Hey, Happy, Where can I get bug lures, anyway?"

"You %^&*&^'s found my molding machine, didn't you?!"

"What molding machine, Happy?" I say. "Oh, you mean the one under the rags in back?"

"You %^&*&^'s!"

'Course, after Arturo leaves I confess: "Arturo was snooping around, that's what happened."

****

Somehow the crowd at Dilly's found out Happy was trying to hide something (I told them), so naturally they latched onto it and spread around the secret. Dan Libby, maybe you know him, from Boonetown, drives all over, some state job, Butterfly Inspector or some fool thing, really is a fly fisherman, it turns out.

Friday. Dan stops by the station. "Hey, Happy, you know, I've got an Easy-Shot machine, just like you! What molds you got?" he asked.

Happy's pouting about all this, but he knows Dan is sometimes a customer, and there ain't that many customers, 'cause we're known as grease goons, and not in the good sense, but maybe I'm being too honest here.

Happy: "Don't have many molds, Dan." Pretends he's busy, but he was loafing, really.

"Why dint you tell me you fly-fished, we can throw a line into Palmer's Creek, I know there's Rainbows...."

Happy: "Oh, I don't fish. I'm making some lures for my friend, my cousin...just helping him out, doesn't know about machinery."

Dan goes over to the Easy-Shot.

"Oh, you got the Jumbo Mayfly, Juicy Cricket...they come with the machine. What's this? Fuzzy Bee, #2. Hey, the only fish that takes these are Hacklehead Bass, they're only in Vermont, you know."

"That's where my cousin's from... Vermont. He asked for the bees."

"Oh, wait, I mean Hacklebacks, they're only in Illinois..."

I picked up some of the little plastic bees he'd made. "You know what? I just had a crazy idea! Suppose you had a flowered dress, you could attach these bees on the dress and then they'd look so natural.... make the flowers seem so real..."

Happy grabs the bees. "Gimme them...you %$#$&%&'s!"

Dear Reader, being a gentleman, I will not repeat the vulgar names Happy called me and poor Dan. Happy stamped his feet, rather reminding me of Rumplestiltskin, but I refrained from mentioning the resemblance.

He told us both to "Git, git, git." So we did. Maybe he meant I was fired from my lucrative job, but perhaps not, as I just went back to work the next day and pretended I knew nothing about his puppy-dog infatuation with our fair and ditzy neighbor.

****

Things were pretty quiet for some days. No calls from my whiney sister. Hoss Wiley brought over his rust-bucket Fordson hoping we could do a miracle and cure the stalling and smoke symptoms. I cleaned the plugs, which Henry Ford must have sold to him personally, but no good result from that. Happy shimmed the valve lifters with pennies and then it ran with a new wheezy sound. "Wheeezy--shoooo....wheeezy-shoo..." Like that at idle, maybe you've heard that sound... it's not good.

"Rev her up, Hoss, while I squirt this alchy!" hollers Happy. The backfires made me lose my "Space Girls" game right there.

We took a break to have a Ma's Root Beer, when out by the pumps there arose such a clatter, we sprang from our milk crates to see what was the matter!

A decrepit Willys pickup lurched into view, sounding worse than Hoss's junker of a tractor. It was towing what was next to hove into view of our wondering eyes.

Dear Reader, imagine for a moment that Napoleon's wife Josephine had more knowledge of mechanical engineering and organ building than your average empress. Imagine also that one day she says, "Leon, your troops need some entertainment for their march to Moscow! I will convert some hay wagons to play organ music, what do you say? I will make a list of what

194

we need… brass organ pipes, steam boilers, gilt paint, red paint, blue paint, mirrors, stained glass in many colors, some rubies, opals, zirconium crystals, ivory for keys, candelabras, and little vases for roses….I will call them steam calliopes!"

Dear Reader, imagine now that she prevailed in her quest and one of these marvels has suffered only minor cannon fire and 200 years of weathering, surviving to the present day.....that describes what is now sitting out by our gas pumps.

A lanky personage unfolded himself from the Willys. A tall Abe Lincoln, clean shaven, though.

"Hi fellas, I'm Morty. Pleased to meetcha." We offered him a Ma's. "Have a Ma's? Ain't cold, sorry, cooler's broke."

Morty explains he's acquired this antique calliope from his former employer, who unfortunately went bust and paid people off in goods rather than money. Can we fix it, he asks, can't seem to get it to work at all.

It's for sale, if we're interested, hasn't had any offers yet, seems as if iPods are raising Heck with the steam calliope market share (who knew?).

"Has it been working? Looks like a rust bucket to me," I says, in a kindly way.

Morty says, "This here calliope, it's a genuine Wurlitzer, you know, is worth a lot."

I'm peering in the guts of this contraption, I guess I made a few more comments that you might consider sneering insults if you were sensitive, and eventually then I look up. Morty is gone.

Instead, one of our town cops is standing there.

"Hey, Smitty, what's up?" I inquired.

"Whose Willys truck here? No plates. Not what we like to see."

Happy comes out. "Hey, what's up, that guy Morty took off through the garage back door into the woods!"

Smitty just leaves the ticket on the Willys and has a root beer with us and tells us the circus wagon's a big road violation with those steel-rimmed wagon wheels, so don't run it on the road, no plates on it neither, then he buzzes off.

****

Happy is cussing about this junker wagon blocking the gas pumps. 'Course it ain't that big a deal since both of 'em don't work right now and have "Out of Order" signs, one of those items we have to attend to soon.

Happy is scowling. "Look at this freakish thing. Dented pipes, all corroded and leaking some god-awful oil or sumpin'. Listen, Sherm, call Nate Hashen at the junkyard and git him to come over here and haul this rusty bucket o' bolts OUTTA here!"

So I go to the phone and dial up Nate.

Suddenly, an angel's voice calls from across the road: "Happy! I'm in love with you!"

"I'm coming to kiss you and hug you!"

It's Noodle, out walking her poodle.

"You have a Mighty Wurlitzer! I can't believe my eyes! I love calliopes! It's so beautiful I want to cry!"

Happy, dumbfounded, gets a big hug, and I'm jealous. But Heck, what am I thinking? She's older than me, probably she wouldn't look at me twice. I'm just a kid to her.

"Did you just get it? It's the real thing isn't it....see the nameplate: 1887, Philadelphia! And original pipes! Know how I can tell? It's the little numbers engraved right there... and there. Where'd you get it, Happy?"

"Um, um, yes,.....I don't actually own it yet, looking to buy it, of course."

Happy touches the pipes lovingly, the metal streaked with green corrosion and gray dust. "Sure is a beauty, ain't it? I love those brass pipes!"

****

Nell, my pesky sister, calls me.

"You know, Morty never came back with the game board for the two-headed chicken."

I explained that Morty didn't have license plates and ran away.

"Well, the customers love Betsy-Ellen so we should get the tick-tack-toe game working, too."

197

"He's just abandoned his Willys and the circus wagon, too, you know."

I filled Nell in about that.

"Can you find him, Sherm? He's just trying to skip out on that ticket, probably."

Later, another Nell call, interrupting again. I'm up seven runs against the Baltimore Orioles pinball game. It times out, so hurry up, Nell!

She says, "Funniest thing, I got hold of that Happy-Time Carnival. It ain't out of business, and they never heard of Morty! Never heard of the two-headed chicken or calliope!"

"Nell, I don't care about Morty and his gosh-darn chicken and circus wagon anyways! I got work to do!" (After I win this game.)

****

Next day I pull in early to Happy's. I've been thinking how to fix that muffler on the Reo, where there's nothing available, and we have to wing it. I'll just do the corkscrew like we did on the Nash that time… Whoa, Happy's here already polishing up calliope organ pipes! Got that wreck in Bay #1, and my Reo job out in the lot! Ain't done with the Reo, Boss!

Next minute, who is it but our Noodle! She appears looking fresh and perky and I keep looking at her, even though she's got a few years on me and is a dipsy-doodle of the first order.

I pass on what Nell found out, they never heard of Morty, etc. This concerns Noodle.

"How will you buy the Wurlitzer, then? If you restore it, Mr. H., the owner may return and not sell it after all! We must look everywhere for Morty, and complete the transaction."

"We don't even know his last name, you know," says Happy, unhappily.

Noodle goes out to the Willys that Morty just left here. Fishes in the glove box. What's this? There's an old Happy Times Carnival flyer. One of the pictures is a fire-eater. A tall fellow it is. It's Morty, the string bean! He did work for them, so they're hiding something.

Noodle says, "I have to go now, my friends, my bread is in the oven. Let me think about this problem."

"He'd be pretty dumb to just leave his stuff here, just wait, he'll come back when he thinks Smitty's not around," I said.

In fact, I was prescient indeed. Next day the Willys was gone! Morty must have had an extra key. But the Mighty Wurlitzer was locked in Bay #1.

****

Noodle indeed thought about it. "Gentlemen, I have a little plan. You both can help. We shall find the elusive Morty."

"Mr. H., will you please sit down here, we need you to have an arm cast."

Noodle has scissors and as Happy looks on, bewildered, she snips around his upper right shirtsleeve so he's down to his bare arm. Then she wraps some cloth around his arm and then Plaster of Paris she brought along. I don't think she knows how to make a proper cast, it gets bigger and bigger, like a leg cast, finally, she's done and the plaster is hardening as fast as she trowels it on.

"Now, I did a little research. A nice law enforcement officer in DELETED told me about the Sopwetzes, always trouble, operating without permit, illegal gambling, suspected stolen goods…"

"I stopped by the Snip 'n Talk Beauty Salon in that town, and it wasn't long before I found out a few possibly useful items about Ms. Sopwetz. She comes in quite often and always shops in the local Walrus Mart for groceries on Wednesday. If we hurry, we can get there before 2:00 PM"

The three of us pile in Noodle's Jeep and drive over hill and dale about 60 miles it seems, and park outside the DELETED Walrus Mart.

"Now Mr. H., just go in there, put three watermelons in your cart and make sure you bump into Ms. Sopwetz, a big bump that she'll remember, then apologize and say it's because you broke your arm, the cart has a bad wheel, you're sorry, OK. Go quick, there she is."

"That her, with the white hat?" I ask.

"Yes, did you see her, Mr. H.?"

"No, didn't see, I was looking the other way," said Happy.

Noodle continues, "Never mind, I'll go in and point her out. She has on a white hat. Wait, no, I can't go in, she'll see me..."

"Mr. U., will you go and make sure he hits the right woman? Wait, you need this disguise, we can't let her see your face, you know!" She sticks a fake mustache under my nose and I don dark glasses.

I'm feeling I'm getting into dangerous waters here. What crazy idea has Noodle got anyway? But who can resist those big blue eyes, and she's only slightly older than me.

Now wearing the silly disguise, I head into the store. I'm just in time to see Happy heading for his target in the distance...a lady in a white hat...he's awkward with the giant arm cast...he misses her cart and hits the lady...I hurry closer, Blimey! It's a nun! She does have a white hat, sure.

"OOOW!........ You $%&#&$$!!" says Ms. Nun, "You want that other arm busted, too?"

Oh my. Happy apologizes, as well he might. I apologize to her, too, which doesn't make any sense since I was nowhere near when it happened. Suddenly I see Target Lady, Ms. Sopwetz... next aisle over.

"Psst, Happy, there she is," I whisper, and then I take a great interest in some shriveled fish in the seafood case.

Off goes Happy, but this woman is a fast shopper and heads down the next aisle, Happy speeds down the other side and bangs into some heads of lettuce, knocking them all over.

Now Happy's going south while Ms. Sopwetz is going north, a game of chicken. Bam! Mission accomplished. "OWWH! You &%^$&* idiot! Dummkopf!" One of Happy's big watermelons rolls out and breaks on the floor. A store person, probably the manager, runs up…. "Sir! Sir! Are you having trouble controlling your cart?"

Happy points to his big cast and mumbles more apologies, and he wisely decides not to purchase any watermelons after all, but rather does a brisk walk for the door. So do I.

Luckily, Noodle has the getaway Jeep running and we hop in and squeal outta there.

"How'd it go, Mr. H.? Did you bump into Ms. Sopwetz?"

"Yep. No problem," says Happy, modestly. He tries to clean off the gobs of watermelon from his shoe.

****

Noodle has her Saaz Naatz class Thursday, so it isn't till Friday we set out again.

An assortment of carnival trucks and rides are parked pell-mell in a hilly field south of DELETED. We drive across more or less roadless ground and eventually find a small trailer-office labeled with a small sign: "Sopwetz".

We surmise this to be the central command of Happy Times Carnival, Inc., Tverso and Svenrina Sopwetz, Owners.

Our knock is answered by: "Enter pleece!"

Ms. Sopwetz puffed on her cigar and scowled. Mr. Sopwetz, completely bald and also smoking a cigar, didn't look up at all, just was busy feeding crackers to an ugly little dog that sat on his desk in the middle of many papers and folders.

Our leader, Noodle, enthuses, "Happy Times is a great show, Ms. S., and we're hoping to join you. That's why we came. Perhaps you have heard of us, we're pretty well known, I'm Madame Grasfoss, the Green Light Psychic, and this is my assistant, Mr. Pulaski!"

Ms. S. did not seem impressed, but on the other hand did not shoo us out the door. Noodle told me on the way over Ms. S. was a believer in fortune-telling. Everybody at Snip 'n Talk Beauty Salon knew it. Our trump card.

Noodle, of course, has an entire Gypsy loose-fitting dress and headscarf, and many beads and bracelets. She continues in a confidential voice, "I have the gift, you know, no fakery."

"I work with the crystal and Mr. Pulaski is my lightning rod. He has a wonderful gift for collecting the energy that is all around us and it flows from him with the help of a light source. We have found green light of a certain frequency is the best..."

"Dearie, I'm very busy, we vant no vortuna tallers, it's no draw no more... ve did haf onct...but..."

Ms. Sopwetz was not so receptive. Will we get the job? What if we do get the job? What am I doing here, anyway?

Noodle pulls out a pretty large crystal ball from an embroidered bag and peers into it. "Mr. Pulaski, just a little stream of the green light, please." I show the flashlight rig on the glass ball. It has a faint swirling fog effect inside.

"Ahh…I love to see the swirling shapes…. would you put your hand on the crystal Ms. S.?"

She does.

"Ahh… I see a scene from your past, it is an industrial city, you are very young… I see great iron ships, the city's name starts with…a 'G'?"

"Gdansk!" says Ms. S. "I grew up right by the shipyards!"

Noodle is getting warmed up: "Look, it is a very recent thing…you are in a store…it is amusing. I see <u>large round objects, green</u>… wait, there is a <u>collision</u>… a person with a <u>big white arm</u>… he bumps into you and you were briefly angry due to this amusing incident…"

Ms. S. leans forward, takes the cigar and waves it a bit…"Not so amusing, I t'ink, but you are right…Just this week it was… a stupid crazy man hits me with his cart!"

"Tverso, come here, she can really see things, her husband helps to bring the visions!"

"I see many things, many times it's the <u>unusual</u> that comes into view….wait there's something…recently you gave a wagon… a generous gift…a strange farm wagon, painted bright colors, it has a load of vertical sticks, no, they are metal, and it has big spoked wheels. Did you give some-body a wagon with big wheels, Ms. Sopwetz?"

"Why…ve did have such a vagon…."

"Oh. Oh, now Mr. Pulaski, bring the light closer...I see something shiny and valuable hidden in the wagon..."

"Very strange... the wagon has black and white, black and white in a row, it is like a picket fence, but lying flat, a very small fence..."

Ms. S. is out of her chair and looking into the misty globe.. "No, it is piano keece, it is a calliope, you see...for playing the pipes..."

"Ah, perhaps it is so, and under these keys, there are ...bright yellow disks, many there are, wait, move the green light ...breath deeply Mr. Pulaski. Now it's clearer, ah.. gold coins!.. hundreds, thousands.. And they have been hidden so long I see they are surrounded by the mists of time...the coins are talking to me...We are here! We are here!"

Noodle sits back in her chair. "I must rest a moment..." Then she peers some more. "I see something else here, it is the future this time... leaky pipes, water, oh, no, it is electricity that is leaking, and the big generator has lost all the electricity and the carnival lights get dimmer and dimmer...it is in the future, ten days, twenty days from now, expensive repairs will be needed, I'm sorry to tell this bad news..."

Ms. S.: "Stop, enough of the bad news. That I can predict myself, hah!"

"Madame Grasfoss, I t'ink you are good as you say, but...we must t'ink this over, can't hire nobody you know right quick, leaf your business card if you pleece."

We make our exit and then the good payoff: We stay out of sight and before long the carnies go to Morty's place looking for the calliope. We tail their old Buick, and sure enough, they drive a few miles and stop at a woodsy driveway and pull off the road, get out and go sneaking toward a trailer in the woods.

They're sneaking up on Morty's place, probably thinking to grab the (non-existent) coins without telling Morty anything. 'Course the calliope isn't there and they knock on the door, and Morty isn't there either. But his name is on the mailbox, "Mortimer Callahan".

Success! We found Morty!

So we head back to the garage. Nell is there.

Nell: "By the way, I looked in the phone book and found Morty, and called him. He'll sell the calliope, $300."

Us undercover investigators didn't know what to say, really.

****

If you're still with me, Dear Reader, you'll agree that about here things look good for those who admire and desire steam calliopes, however, the last word has yet to be spoken in that regard.

Before any such transaction of $300 could take place, the ever-alert DELETED Valley police force, in the person of Officer Finn Smith informed us that several items had been recently stolen from a show operator in Florida, namely the very same Wurlitzer calliope and also Betsy-Ellen, the two-headed chicken sensation. No doubt that would explain why the

Sopwetzes said they never heard of Morty, since they either stole the things or knew they were hot goods.

So these items must be returned to their rightful owners, and I don't mind that development, I confess, because, listen, I'm telling you, if Happy buys that calliope (junk wagon) I may end up with some disagreeable organ pipe polishing that could last probably the rest of my life, if I live that long, and cut into my pinball time by a lot, a lot.

The peace and quiet I hoped for didn't prevail for long.

Happy made the mistake of stopping by Dilly's for coffee the next day with the big Frankenstein arm cast. I heard a report from Arturo.

"It's nuthin'," says Happy when, of course, people asked what's wrong with his arm.

"Workin' on an engine, kinda hurt m'arm."

'Course, he's pretending he's not ga-ga over Noodle. Can't let on that he's been helping her out with crazy schemes like he was. Well, I was, too, but only 'cause he's my boss, so, oh Heck, yeah, I'm a little tiny bit drawn to the fair lady, I s'pose, so there, if you want to know.

Happy's cussin' when I got to work. "Couldn't work these blasted tin snips with m'left hand, y'know, so I had to sleep with this thing, it's like a log on yer stomach," he says.

"Here, I got the Sawsall right here," I volunteered.

Grumble, grumble, grumble. Wouldn't let me do it quick with

the power saw, he just chipped timidly with a dull chisel for hours.

Then his shirt's only got one sleeve, like half his brain wants to be a biker, but the other half normal garage mechanic.

****

Calliope didn't go away. Officer Smith told us more about the owners of the calliope. Seems these Florida folks didn't have a carnival, but they wanted to and were rounding up the proper equipment that you needed for a carnival. They at present were running an establishment known as Rolly Bowly, a two-lane bowling alley and roller-skate rental place. Why the skate rental? During certain hours you could skate up and down the alleys.

Unfortunately, Rolly Bowly, Inc. was going bankrupt due to a slump in the market for bowling and rolling in that part of the Florida swamps. Sheriff G. said they seemed to have moved with no forwarding address. If we hear from them, let him know, because there are a few bill collectors and a district attorney that would like to talk with them.

One good thing. Noodle talks to Nell. Why not put the Mighty Wurlitzer by the Two Pigs Cave entrance, while we're waiting for the owners to take it back? Nell says, yes, a nice objet d'art. Too bad it's not actually working.

Nell says, "Shouldn't be too hard to fix it, do'ya think?" I says, "Yeah, well while we're at it let's go to Egypt and bring some of those mummies back to life."

So Noodle sweet talks Officer Smith into allowing the road-destroying iron tires to travel once again. Happy tows the thing to the cave. Bay #1 can now be used for regular business.

****

Do I now get to go back to my career of mechanic's helper at a backwater garage in the decaying township of DELETED Valley? No, not yet. Nell has just this one thing to ask.

"Shermy, you know while we're waiting for the owners of Betsy-Ellen to show up, we could be making a few bucks, patrons see this setup and want to play the game. You know about how things work, come on and help us figure it out."

So it comes to pass I'm stopping over to the cave next morning. I brought over a box of sticky buns for everybody.

Turns out Morty is there. He thought he might get some work at the cave. He's kind of lost. He went back to see the carnies (Sopwetz family) but the whole field was empty and so he's still stiffed for his back pay. But he's cheerful enough, like it's what you expect working for carnies.

Nell says to Morty, the string bean, "What can you do? Can you operate this chicken game and make money?"

I pipe up, "Well, that's a great idea, Morty. You take over on the chicken problem. I have to get back to the garage, got a lube, oil, and filter to do on a Hudson, you know."

But...we learn that Morty, when he worked at Happy Time, did fire-eating and juggling flaming torches and never even saw the two-headed chicken until they gave it to him instead of real cash money, so he just brought over the game board and put stuff in place with the booth and all. Didn't know the deal. The chicken just was hanging around ignoring the interesting and colorful tick-tack-toe game board. Stolen two-headed chicken tick-tack-toe carnie booths don't come with instructions.

About then a rusty panel truck pulls into view. The tailpipe is dragging. Faded graphics on the side, bowling pins, (AMF's), 'Rolly Bowly Lanes' in big yellow letters. Mr. and Ms. Irving Bobwick emerged. Their clothes were rumpled, there were bags under their eyes, Mr. Bobwick needed a shave; it looked like they'd been driving day and night from Florida.

"We've been driving day and night from Florida!" said Ms. Bobwick.

Nevertheless, they weren't too tired to admire Nell's cave and wanted to know all about it, and of course Nell gave them a tour, and fed them coffee and my sticky buns. They said the cave was really wonderful, and Nell instantly liked these birds (fly-by-nights).

The real owners of Betsy-Ellen had now arrived and I can tell you it was a touching reunion. It was a happy Betsy-Ellen now, puck-puck-puck to beat the band. Nell said before, she looked despondent, moody, just pecked at her food.

Fiona Bobwick did some quick adjustments and got things lighting up on the tick-tack-toe board. Betsy-Ellen pecked judiciously, beating Nell three times!

"I'll just finish this coffee and get back to the garage," I said, easing my way toward the door.

Fiona is saying to Nell, "You know, Irv and I are going to have our own traveling carnival, but while we get things lined up on that, we could use an income stream. Why don't we operate the Betsy-Ellen concession right here? It would add some interest to your place here, of course, just until Irv and I put together our traveling carnival."

Nell says OK. Nell had second thoughts pretty soon, though. The Bobwicks parked their panel truck in the woods nearby and camped out in it. They did their laundry in the Perpetual Stream getting soapsuds in it, and hung a clothesline between some stalactites before Nell stopped them.

For my part, I head out, hoping not to hear any more about calliopes or chickens. Will I get my wish? Do dandelions grow at Augusta National Golf Course?

****

Somehow, Nell has got some school groups to visit the cave, and calls for help to manage these flocks on those days. Pendergast has hurt his arm falling out of a tree (or off a bar stool), so he's now a tour guide until he can be an apple picker again.

I show up to help, too. A troop of girl scouts is there crowded around looking at Betsy-Ellen. Fiona is doing her carnie spiel.

As you know by now, the cave's boring, so people prefer to gawk at the two-headed chicken and play the tick-tack-toe game.

I'm having a coffee at one of the outdoor tables and I overhear a couple of girls, about nine years old.

"Listen, Annie, I've watched and studied this chicken game ….got it pegged…I sneaked behind and there's some little lights that reflect toward the bird that cue it to which square to peck! It's a scam!"

"Good work, Milly!"

"I see how to foil it, too…just give me a minute, let me have those fingernail clippers of yours." They take off back to the booth.

This has me curious, so I follow them back over.

"Oh, I've lost my quarters!" cries Annie. She gets Fiona to help look down on the ground, and in a blink, Milly ducks under the booth curtain, pretending to help search.

The fussing and commotion is soon over, and I pretend to be arranging the chairs so I can hear some more.

They're whispering, but I still can hear. "I cut the wire, Annie!… no more cue lights…let's see how smart that chicken is now!"

The other kids have used up their dollars so Milly gets to be next to play. Milly hands over her dollar, Betsy-Ellen moves first as per the rules. Always goes to the center square, it seems.

Milly moves. Betsy-Ellen does nothing. Fiona pokes her, she pecks a square. A few moves later, Milly wins!

Fiona can't believe it. She strokes and picks up Betsy-Ellen, giving a little pep talk, I guess. Milly hops excitedly and picks out one of the prizes that never get won, a large fluffy teddy bear.

Milly plays again, wins again! Fiona tries to rally Betsy-Ellen… like a boxing second, a rubdown, a drink of water.

Doesn't work. Betsy-Ellen is on the ropes…pecks randomly. But then things stop. The girls have used up all their money.

Milly comes over to me. "Say, mister, I can win a prize for you if you give me a dollar."

I give her several ones. "Sure, kid, here….and you can keep the prizes." I head back to the garage.

****

Back at the garage, the income stream is less than a rushing torrent. Both bays are empty.

I'm standing way inside Bay #1. I've got one end of a long tape measure. "Stand there, next to the tire machine," says Happy. He walks backwards straight out past the gas pumps and is in the middle of the road before he stops.

"Forty-three feet right here!" he hollers.

"Boss, get outta the road!" says I.

"If we take that fire engine job, that's where it'll be, out in the road. Think anybody'll complain? Forty-eight feet to the end of the ladder."

Happy, scowling, mumbles on, "We need the work. I'll call the station and tell 'em to send it over. Bubba says it runs, but there's a lot of blue smoke, you know."

"Boss, that's a Cummins diesel, and we got no injector tools, y'know."

Phone rings. Nell.

"Irv Bobwick's going to stop by to borrow a couple of tools, OK, isn't it? He says the calliope was actually working when they had it, but it's got a little rust and he just has to take apart some of the steam valves and so on, but then…"

"Nell, you know we got a lot to do, big fire engine job, we'll need all our tools, I think you have to tell this Irv fella no dice. I can tell you right now, Irv has got to get his own $&%#$%$& tools, he's a moocher and we'd never get 'em back."

Nell continues, "Noodle's going to come over and would love to hear it going…it has John Phillip Sousa marches, and it has a manual keyboard, it's automatic or you can play the keyboard. Noodle is a musician, you know, has written dozens of songs, jazz, the hardest thing to write."

"Well, Nell… maybe just a few tools, if he promises to bring 'em back."

Noodle is, after all, a newcomer to DELETED Valley. I should get to know her, make her feel welcome. Least I can do for a neighbor. She's about my age, I think.

I was at the cave working on the Incredible Tiny Man Skeleton exhibit. (Squirrel bones, actually. Don't tell Nell I told you.) Who walks in but Mr. Sopwetz! Easy to spot: short, shiny bald head and he's smoking a big black cigar like before. Apparently he didn't recognize me as the fortune teller assistant without my fake mustache and dark glasses. He's snooping around the calliope! Hah! Asks Nell if it's for sale, acts as though he's an antique collector. I walk up.

With a big smile I boom out, "You know it's real interesting what we found! You wouldn't believe it! GOLD COINS!, thousands, right under the keyboard, right there, you see?

Mr. Sopwetz gaped, dropping his cigar. His eyes bulged out. "AEEEIII!!!" he declared.

"Yeah," I continued, "worth $1.3 million dollars!"

"OWWWWEEEUUII!" he said.

Mr. S. sat down on a bench and looked into space, shaking his head in a jittery kind of way.

I continue, "If you want to buy this calliope, just talk to the owner, Mr. Bobwick, he's out front right now, painting the chicken booth. See right there, through the window?"

"Bobwick?? Where?"

Perhaps not wanting to talk to the man he stole the stuff from, I suppose, he moves to leave somehow other than the front way.

The perceptive Mr. Bobwick now spots Baldy, then comes running.

"Sopwetz, you thief! I knew it was you before I heard from police, Swine!...stole Betsy-Ellen, stole my Wurlitzer...in the night you crept like a creep!"

"Bobwick! It is you at fault... you owed me! You sold to me broken equipment...the Whirley-Wheel was broke...Bobwick, get away from me with your paintbrush..."

"I'll paint hair on your bald head! I've got black right here...you want to look young, don't you?..... A beard, too, maybe, Sopwetz?"

Mr. Sopwetz was quick enough to avoid that embarrassment, lurching through some surprised customers to his car. He drove away without even saying goodbye to us. A paintbrush bounced off his car.

Order Now!

The boss, Bev, was young with movie star good looks. I answered a tiny job ad and the place was a dump in a rust-belt neighborhood, but one look at her and I knew I would take the job, whatever it was. Why wasn't she married? "I'm waiting for Mr. Last Resort. He would be a heavy drinker and gambler, have a pot belly and bald head. Where am I going to find him?" she lamented.

She was always looking for new thingydoodles to peddle. It was a mail-order joint, The DELETED, DELETED Company of DELETED, Inc. Everything strictly legal, of course, just liked to keep a low profile. We never invited Mike Wallace to stop by, for example.

One morning Bev came to my desk and pushed the clutter aside to make room for her coffee and sat down. "Alvin, we are on the rocks," she said, helping herself to a bite of my doughnut. "Look at these sales figures," she continued, as she dumped them in the waste basket. "All dogs lately!"

"What samples came in today? Will we ever find anything that people will buy? What do you have there?"

"It's a stupid dinner plate that can spin around on a little bearing," I said, "called a Platteroozie."

"I hate it already!"

"The description says it's all the rage in fashionable dining. Adds variety and flair to plain things. For example, you can make twirly patterns in mashed potatoes as you spin the Platteroozie. And if you put peas on it they would arrange themselves in a perfect circle around the rim. And how convenient it is to simply rotate your different food items for easy access."

"Humph. It's useless."

"But Bev, all of our products are useless."

"Oh yeah, I forgot, I forgot. Put it on the ad list."

****

I took the mail-order job to earn some money. My life's work, up to that point, had been my Electrophoresis Hypnosis Projector, or EHP.

"If that thing hypnotizes me, you can have the rest of my jelly doughnut!" said Bev.

I set the controls for Test No.1, which is to make the subject act like a chicken, whenever I say "cigar".

"Are you relaxed, Bev?"

"Yes, just go already."

"MWERMREWWWWWWWWWWWWEEEEERRRP!"

"Now what, Svengali?"

"Now we wait for me to say the special word."

"OK, OK, I've got orders to fill, not many, but…"

"Cigar."

"What?"

"Cigar."

"See, Mr. Edison. No jelly doughnut."

"You don't feel like….saying anything or acting in a different way?"

"No. Say, Alvin, have you got a cigar?"

"Neither of us smokes cigars, Bev. Funny, though, I could go for a cigar, myself. I'll go down to the corner and get some."

I got back and we lit up. "PUFF, PUFF, PUFF." "PUFF, PUFF, PUFF."

"Bev, I think the emission coils are not tuned just right, PAWK! PAWK! PAWK!"

I flapped my wings. "PAWK! PAWK! PAWK!"

"PAWK! PAWK! PAWK!" I pecked at the tuner dial. "PUK-PUK-PUK! We'll try it again tomorrow, Bev."

****

Monday. I found a huge combat boot by the road. Brought it in to work. I did a little work with hammer and nails and made a kind of drop hammer.

"BAM! BAM! BAM!" "I hope this noise isn't bothering you, Bev."

I attached the boot filled with rocks and some railroad spikes to a pivoting board.

"Alvin, I know a very good psychiatrist, Dr. Pavlov. Why don't I make an appointment for you?"

"Not him again, with the bell routine! Lousy snacks, too, tasted like dog biscuits!"

The hard part was attaching the pulley to the ceiling. But Alvin doesn't give up. Perspired a bit, it was hot in DELETED. "See, Bev, I said. "Lift it with the rope and let go." It would drop about six feet to the floor making a very satisfactory "STOMP!" noise.

From my desk I picked up a little plastic gnome happily waving his arm. I placed him in the drop zone.

"I think it is our duty to thoroughly test products before we offer them to the public, don't you, Bev?"

"CRUNCH!!!"

"This one failed, I'm afraid."

Companies are constantly sending us samples, trying to sucker us into marketing their tin and plastic loser products. I was going through Monday's deliveries and found a rare good one.

"Hey, Bev, here's a sure winner. 'UNCLE DELETED'S MOSQUITO FARM' I'll read the instructions to you."

"Watch families of happy mosquitoes in their own swamp home of rotting wood and muck."

"See them teaching their cute children how to use their proboscis to suck blood. Place Mom's or Dad's or an expendable friend's bare arm against the farm opening labeled 'Mosquito Feeding Window'."

"You can tell male from female by observing anatomical features..."

"Bev, some of this I'm too embarrassed to read out loud."

"CAUTION! Do not open the cover for observation, as the mosquitoes may get out."

"We can take a quick peek, can't we?" I said.

"Hmmmmmmmmmmmmmmmm, hmmmmmmmmmm, SLAP! SLAP ! SLAP!   SLAP ! SLAP! SLAP ! Hmmmmmmmmm mmmmmmmm,   hmmmmmmmmmm,

SLAP! SLAP ! SLAP!   SLAP ! SLAP! SLAP !"

"Bev, I think this is a sure winner!"

"Hmmmm   mmmmmm   mmmmm   mmmmmm
mmmmm,   hmmmmmmmmm,   SLAP!   SLAP   !
SLAP! SLAP ! SLAP! SLAP !"

"They even have a nice tie-in: *UNCLE DELETED'S MOSQUITO BITE SALVE, Sold separately.*"

"Great! Put it on our ad list, Alvin, that will sell big!" Bev said.

****

For hypnosis to work, you have to soften up the subject. For example, show someone a one-week-old kitten. "Awwww, how cute," they'll say.

They are lulled and tranquil. Then you hit them with the hypnotic suggestion.

I bought three kittens at Millie's Pet Shop. Three cute girls from the local college were in there and couldn't resist petting and cuddling them. We got to talking and I explained about my Electrophoresis Hypnosis Projector.

That's how come a certain gorgeoso blonde named Wendy showed up at our cluttered office at quitting time. She had languid dreamy hazel eyes and smooth straight hair, and a beautiful smile.

Was I so fickle I was paying more attention to Wendy than to

Bev? Yes. She was a psychology major, with an interest in hypnosis.

"Alvin, show me how your special machine works!" she said.

"Sure, I'll set it up. This time, I'll try the 'REVEAL PROMP-TER' function. Hypnosis may assist a person in getting in touch with their deeper feelings."

"Are you relaxed, Wendy?"

"I'm relaxed."

"Is your chair comfy?"

"Yes, comfy."

"Would you hold this little kitten for me?"

"Awwww, how cute!"

"MWERMREWWWWWWWWWWWWEEEEERRRP!"

"So, Wendy, what do you feel like right now, happy, sad, indifferent?"

Wendy: "I feel happy, in fact, I could sing a song. What song? I don't know, maybe...."

Wendy got up and held her hands out to hush the audience of two and sashayed into **"Blue Skies"**! What a voice! What exuberance! Bev started to sing, too. Wendy finished that and said, "Doesn't that make you want to smile?.......Smile???"

"Bev, what am I doing?"

"Smiling."

"Alvin, what am I doing?"

"Smiling."

Then she went right into **"When You're Smiling"**! In the middle, the UPS man, Jared, came in and joined in. Nice voice. Probably doesn't do many singing deliveries.

Even I, Alvin Frog-voice sang along, even though I hardly knew the words. Wendy wrapped that up and said, "Doesn't that just make you happy?.....Happy???"

Guess what, she started right in on **"I Want to Be Happy"**.

Halfway through, Jennie delivered the pizza we had ordered and she sang, too, holding the pizza box above her head and spinning around!

Wendy would have continued, but we all realized the phone had been ringing, ringing, ringing, so everybody kind of slowed to a stop. It was a wrong number.

"Are we all trapped in some Off-Broadway musical revival?" asked Bev.

"God works in mysterious ways, but I think it's just an ordinary Electrophoresis Hypnosis Projector effect," I said.

Jennie said, "What's scheduled for tomorrow?"

Friday. More complaints: (a famous billionaire) says he got the "Complete Earthworm Business Kit", but no starter worms. Can't he go outside with a shovel? Complaints. (another famous billionaire): He's happy with the Disappearing Ink, but the Magic Dollar Bill Machine wasn't what he expected. Brigadier General DELETED: Wrong color bunny slippers.(Didn't I already tell him we were out of pink?) Queen DELETED returned the book: How to Beat the House at Vegas; didn't beat the house, lost her crown, (her Sunday Best one). You can't please everybody.

More samples. I opened up "Conversation Cue Cards For Rube Man".

"These are great, Bev. For the young man who hasn't done that much socializing, not confident in various situations."

"You mean a yokel, like you?"

"Bev...be nice. Say the young man is with a lady. He's stuck for something to say. Just peeks at a card as needed, she's impressed. Product of China, so the translations may not be perfect."

"The first category is 'At the Dancing'."

"Card 1. Do you prance now or ever again?
Card 2. My heart wobble upon the music, also you chick?
Card 3. Waltz can happen with me or Fox-Will-Trot, too.
Card 4. Is a rock-a-roll for you?"

"Another category, 'At the Sand Beach'."

"Card 1. ZahZoom! Nice features, dear.
Card 2. Care for lotion, every body part?"

"Bev, I can't read the rest in a family story, OK?"

"Story?"

"Never mind, Bev."

"Another category, 'Orders at Feed Trough'."

"Card 1. A grape vino, one gallon missie, one gallon myself, too.
Card 2. A steak victual, char to crisp.
Card 3. A salad of green leaves, maple.
Card 4. Two best dessert, Honey Pie."

"See, Bev, the girl is surprised, the guy from the farm knows his way around!"

"You're right, Alvin, put it on our ad list. Let me read the rest of that part 'At the Sand Beach'."

****

Across the hall in our building was the Repo Man, a gruff character, Grigori Rasputin. We'd sometimes meet in the hall. Rumored to be an ex-con.

He came in to borrow cigars, and asked about the strange machine. Turns out he had a stutter. Could we cure it? I said, "Sure."

I set up the machine tuned for a trance mode that should be good for behavior modification.

"MWERMREWWWWWWWWWWWWEEEEERRRP!"

"Repeat after me Grigori, 'I WILL NOT STUTTER!'."

"I WILL NOT S-S-STUTTER!"

"Again."

"I WILL NOT STUTTER!"

"Good. Now say: 'I AM AN UGLY EX-CON, BUT I DON'T STUTTER!'."

"I AM AN UGLY EX-CON, BUT I DON'T STUTTER!"

He was in a trance. I whispered to Bev that just for fun I was tuning for 'REVEAL' mode.

"MWERMREWWWWWWWWWWWWEEEEERRRP!"

"Say, Grigori, do you have any SECRETS…just between you and me?"

"Oh, sure, like where I hid the loot from the McCracken job…it's under the McCracken family headstone! Ha, ha, ha.! I'll get it when the heat is off."

"Oh really, ha, ha, ha, you fooled them that time!"

While I talked to Grigori, Bev phoned the Sixth Precinct. They were quite interested in what Mr. Rasputin had to say. They relayed a few items to ask about.

"Say, Grigori, know anything about that Collins heist?"

In fact, he himself had pulled it off, assisted by a certain Mr. Buster Kelly.

"Hey, where is Buster, now?"

"You know Buster? Why, he's hiding out at Room 56, Hotel Royale, Toronto, 453-421-8953."

"Hey, I'll have to give the old son-of-a-gun a ring!"

After a few more interesting notes from the underworld, Mr. Rasputin left a happy, non-stuttering man. Didn't see him after that, though. The Sixth Precinct folks may have had some follow-up questions.

****

"Bev, this toad doesn't hop worth a darn."

"What toad?"

"Tippity Toppity Hoppity Floppity Toad is his full name, probably 'Wimp' to his friends."

I wound him up as tight as he went. "Buzz! Blip! Bzzz! Blip! Bz."

"Very feeble hops, Bev, this is not even up to the low standards of DELETED, DELETED Company of DELETED, Inc."

Then I remembered Mr. Skolnik's anti-gravity popcorn! In high school I had a secret after-school job helping him in his underground workshop. A ruby laser at the right frequency would flip the starch molecules to the anti-gravity state. I took notes on the whole deal.

"Bev, it's your lucky day. I need to get some apparatus together, then things will really be hopping around here."

"This doesn't involve combat boots, does it?"

What fun! I worked evenings in one of the storerooms. Surplus Mart laser, popcorn popper, hotplate cooker. On Wednesday I popped a big batch. Thursday I showed Bev. "Watch this, Bev!"

I opened the pot lid and all the popcorn shot to the ceiling and stayed there!

Naturally, she saw how this would help our wimpy toad friends. I modestly named this material "Alvin 1", or "A1" for short. Of course, I should have named it after the inventor, Mr. Skolnik, but he wasn't around. Tough popcorn, Mr. Skolnik.

Indeed, when packed with A1, Hoppity made huge hops, bouncing off the ceiling each time. More like it.

After playing with the toads awhile, I got back to handling the mail.

We get a lot of complaints. Here's one from Prisoner No. DELETED, DELETED State Prison. He bought our handy home study course "Locksmithing Fundamentals". "Disappointing results so far," he says. I wrote back recommending the advanced course.

I opened one of the sample boxes: It was electric erasers for kids, battery operated.

"Bev, Look." I held up Boo-Boo Bunny. Furry and looked sort of like a bunny. Not that much like a bunny. OK, it looked nothing like a bunny unless a furry tube of toothpaste looks like a bunny.

I read from the box: "She erases with her little pink nose, and says 'Boo-Boo' each time. Eraser Rat has an ink eraser nose, and says 'Dumb Kid' each time."

"Bev, this could be one of our best sellers!"

"Alvin, this is a very stupid product. Put it on our ad list along with all the other stupid products."

"Let me have Boo-Boo for a minute, Alvin." "BZZZZZZ! BOO-BOO! BZZZZZZZZ! BOO-BOO!"

"Teachers will ban these idiot talking erasers! We'll get complaints asking for refunds."

"But our policy is to never give refunds, Bev."

"Oh, that's right, I forgot. Who cares, then."

We went for a break at the coffee shop. We were sitting having coffee and talking when along came this gawky guy.

"Hi Bev! How are you?"

He gave Bev a big hug!

"Henry, well, I'll be darned. Do you have the engagement ring with you?"

"No."

"Oh, that's right, you didn't propose to me yet. First things first, I guess."

"Alvin, this is my old friend Henry. He worked at the marina I used to have."

We shook hands. He had a fishy handshake and looked like a young Don Knotts. What's he doing hugging my Bev? She invited him to sit down! Oh, nooo. Get lost, Buddy!

Bev said, "It's really remarkable, you two look so much alike! Don't you think?"

"What is she saying?" I thought, "I'm 20, this geek looks like 16. I have a strong chin, he has a guppy chin, I have a scar above my right eye,... hmmm, he has a scar above his right eye, that's funny."

"Henry, here, has many talents you know. He wrote a whole musical!"

Oh, whoop de doo, Scarface, a musical.

"Many songs. I remember one about the end of summer, sweet and sad, made me cry...'When the Golden Days of Summer Fade to Fall'."

Oh, spare me, what treacle!

"What else have you written, Henry?" gushed Bev.

"Well, I have written a book of short stories, but it's nothing, really."

Oh, nothing, really,....he says. Give me a break from the false modesty!

The unwanted visitor had to get back to work, and we returned to work, also.

"I last time I saw Henry, he was speeding away in an inboard speedboat. I thought I'd never see him again."

"Maybe he'll keep speeding away."

"Alvin, you're not jealous, are you? And here I thought you had your eye on Wendy since she appeared," she said, with her big coy smile.

"Musical. Stories. You know, I've been thinking of writing something myself, just didn't happen to mention it," I said.

"That's great, Alvin, what are you going to write?"

"Maybe about....an old hotel, a faded glory...maybe a marina. A handsome young man comes along, gets a job....the female owner is a genteel beauty, still young but somewhat older than the newcomer, kind of ditzy, worried about being a faded rose..."

"Ditzy?? Faded?? Dumb story so far, Alvin."

****

Bev really liked Wendy and hired her to help out, a part-time job, since she was still in college. Of course I was delighted. Plus, she helped with some of my hypnosis experiments. Got the bubble gum urge along with Bev and me.

She was helping with the mail one Thursday, answering complaints. "I love working here. I'm writing a paper about mail-order marketing psychology, you know," she said.

An uninvited visitor suddenly appeared. "Hello, Henry!" Bev called out.

Oh no. It's the wandering minstrel again. The wimpy fellow greeted us and was introduced to Wendy.

"Just came by to say 'Hi', Bev," he said. "Wendy, I'll probably see you around campus; I'm going to DELETED College, too." "Oh, cool," said Wendy.

What courses? Alphabet 101?

"I've got to get back to work, but I have a suggestion for your business. You should have a BEAUTIFUL GIRL SPOKES-PERSON featured in your ads! It draws attention and gives your company a human face."

Bev said, "Hey, I like it!" Wendy said, "That's good, Henry, people remember faces, not inanimate objects."

"Easy to do, you have two Vogue Cover Girls right here, just pick one! You could call her Ms. DELETED! See how it ties in with your company name DELETED, DELETED Company of DELETED, Inc.?"

"That's a nice pun, Henry, hah, hah, ha," said Bev.

"Haa, ha, ha," Wendy laughed. "That's the funniest pun I ever heard!"

"Well, 'Bye' for now," said Henry.

Not "Bye" for good?

Bev said, "Wendy, you should be Ms. DELETED...."

"Oh, no, Bev, you have such classic good looks, like Drew Barrymore..."

"Oh, don't be silly, you're vivacious and bright, got that young Doris Day look! That's what we need," said Bev.

"What do you think, Alvin?" asked the demur Bev.

"Uh...ummm...I....I think you are both right. Doris day, Drew Barrymore,...exactly."

Then Wendy saved me, saying, "Actually, I won't be able to anyway, you want somebody who will be long-term, not a college kid who may go off any old where after graduation. I appreciate you all thinking of me, though."

The next day, we were doing one of my ongoing hypnosis experiments and Bev and I came away with post-hypnotic preference for year 1900 style of dress. That and a dread of houseflies. That explains why the photos of Ms. DELETED show a beautiful Gibson Girl holding a flyswatter.

****

A couple of weeks later, Bev said, "Alvin, It's been fun to dress with my hair in a bun and all, but the urge is not going away like the cigar smoking."

"I know the feeling, Bev," I said, as I adjusted my straw boater.

"I'm also getting tired of chewing pink bubble gum and wearing roller skates, not to mention the incessant whistling of "Young at Heart", and carrying flyswatters around. I don't suppose you'd like to just drop your idiot hypnosis gadget in the river, would you?"

"Actually, I have a question for you," Bev continued. "Do you have settings on your crackpot machine to make a person really cooperative, helpful, your wish is my command?"

"Yes, I'll just set for Receptive Trance and Cooperation mode."

"Do subjects have to know you're trying to hypnotize them?"

"The invisible beams and low sounds should work whether they know it or not."

"Perfect. See, I want to see if you can point it at strangers, and hypnotize them surreptitiously. Let's go get a coffee at the corner shop and bring your hypnotizer along."

A quick skate brought us to the shop. We plunked down with our coffees, placing the Electrophoresis Hypnosis Projector on the table between us.

"Nice short wave radio, Alvin!" the Boss said, loudly. "Do you have to rotate it to max the reception?"

Then Bev whispered, "See that grouchy guy with the Van Dyke beard? Blast him."

"MWERMREWWWWWWWWWWWWWEEEEERRRP!"

Bev quickly approached the target, asking for the sugar. He stopped frowning and said, "Of course, here, and I'll bring it over, here are the napkins, too. Here's my newspaper, and what else can I do for you? How are you both this morning? You look beautiful, my Dear, and you Sir, you look great, nice outfit and handsome as a prince, here, perhaps you'd like this computer?"

"Thanks so much, but just the sugar is fine."

Beard followed us out of the store like a sheep dog and we had to skate fast and throw garbage cans in his path to shake him.

Out of breath, Bev and I sat for a minute back at the office.

Then, the Boss leaned close to me and said, "Alvin, I think it's time to add a modest <u>retail outlet</u> to The DELETED, DELETED Company of DELETED, Inc."

We looked in the Sub Sub Prime Real Estate Section in the DELETED classifieds. Luckily, one of the dingy boarded-up storefronts near us, on Desolate Avenue (not real name), was available.

We stocked the shelves with thingydoodles from our big storeroom full of dog products known as The Morgue. Soon we opened the doors.

Bev's customers were entertained by Bossa Nova music from an odd-looking radio. At times the lively music was punctuated by this sound:

"MWERMREWWWWWWWWWWWWWEEEEERRRP!"

Bev would invite buyers of one item to consider something more.

She would adjust her 1890's flowery hat, shift her bubble gum and say, "You know, we have some specials today. I'd really be so happy if you would buy, say, this pile of shoddy crap right here!"

The customers always seemed eager for this deal. They also would try to give Bev their purse or wallet, or backpack, or car, which Bev graciously declined to accept.

"Where is this small but prosperous emporium?" you may be asking. Dear Reader, I'll tell you. Just go to DELETED, DELETED in the city of DELETED, DELETED. I myself may not be there, as I am hard at work on my new Gold Sniffer. Would you believe my Electrophoresis Hypnosis Projector combined with a Pocket Hurricane Vac™, (available from DELETED, DELETED Company of DELETED, Inc.,$29.99), can detect GOLD atoms in the air?

Life at Sea

Sam needed a random word to keep his stalled novel moving. Joe closed his eyes and stabbed at the dictionary page with his pencil. "Crossword puzzle," he said.

"That's no good," said Sam. He was stuck after only three chapters of <u>Reggie Danderspoon- Midshipman</u>.

"This is the year 1845, royal navy ship of the line. How am I going to put in a Sunday newspaper pastime?"

"All right, what have you got so far?" said Joe, Sam's pal who sometimes attempted to help such efforts.

"I'll go through it," said Sam, and then he read aloud as follows:

Capt. Chesterfield Woolsley-Granbyshire adjusted his tricorn hat, which as you no doubt know, was standard issue in Her Majesty's Navy for senior officers in the time period of the story you are reading. Namely, 1845 AD.

"Mr. Runfetch, fetch me my spyglass from the quarterdeck goodie locker, there's a good laddie!" barked the captain.

With a weight of only 9-1/2 sqb's (using the old measure of squidbillies, where 1 sqb = 2.567 ounces), this was reliable headwear. The rich felt held its shape well when wet, an important consideration at sea, what with you get now and again squalls and sea spray. And talk about Wash n' Wear! Why, these stalwarts would dry out without a wrinkle! You can see for yourself: simply take a Devonshire Company Tricorn Century II, for example, and get it soaking wet, then place in direct sunlight, (I'm not kidding a bit!) and you will see what I mean. Hey, Skipper, ready to roll again!

…………………..

(Author's note: here space limitations necessitate skipping the rest of Sam's first chapter.)

Chapter The Second

As regards the cost of a Stenthonian Burby Tricorn, let me assure you that 19 shillings, threepence would suffice, except for year-to-year variations due to the periodic shortage of Justinian Wool. Quixotically, it was only available from a high altitude region of the country of Nostalgia which unfortunately is no longer in existence but is sorely missed by many (hence the common word "nostalgia", but I'm sure you knew that).

The 1830's stiff competition for the lucrative tricorn market caused much unrest in Devonshire. Some speculate that the Crimean War was really about dominance of either the tricorn or the duocorn hat! No less a figure than Gladstone (I refer to the prime minister, not the duck) made the "Speech of the Century".....

"Wait, wait, wait,"interrupted Joe. "What's all this about hats?"

"Authenticity, authenticity, Joe,"...said the patient Sam. "Any novelist would tell you...listen, in Chapter The Fourth I get right to his buckle shoes, Tyrolean Cut, Seville leather and....I also include a nice anecdote about how some Second Year Men nailed his shoes to the floor, just before roll call....but.....," Sam trailed off.

"Well, I thought I was getting going in the next chapter, he looks with the brass tube spyglass, a classic meme, y'know. But they are still tied up to the pier, so he looks around, sees Big Ben and remarks it has stopped. Not that exciting.

"That's why I need some kind of input. Crossword puzzle is not a good fit, though."

Joe looked thoughtful for a moment. He wasn't thinking, he just looked thoughtful. Then he said, "Let's re-create the scene, pretend your desk is in the skipper's cabin, located at the aft end of the ship, where the top command plots the course and leads everything. Now why is the command way back there anyway? Couldn't you see better if you were right up at the bow?? Does a fire truck driver sit at the back? Oh, never mind."

Joe continued, "Here, let me write some, Sam, maybe it'll help."

Sam, slumped and tired, waved him a feeble "Go ahead" sign.

Joe started in, " tucca, tucca,…… ticci, tucca….."

"Watcha got there, Booby?" asked the grinning Executive Officer, Lieutenant Smiley.

"It's from my Mum, some cookies and... oooh, the cookies got broken up, look at that! Golly-Gee Hogswoggle, Blame it all Crampity! Excuse my French, Matey."

"Looky here, a big crossword, hey!"

It was a big black and white oilskin tablecloth with a big crossword puzzle, a 15 x 15 one with 2 inch squares. Since it was so big, there was room for the clues in the black squares and around the periphery.

*"An across clue: 'Broadway appendages.' I know '**Gams**'!" burst out the skipper.*

*"And then down is 'Most Resolute': That's '**Gamest**'."*

"Knock, knock, knock." It was their neighbor Silvia. "Say ,. Fellows! I apologize for being slightly sarcastic in the past….calling you dorks and things…., ha, ha, just fun, you know. Here's why I stopped by: Got a new job. Selling for Jokey Joe. It's a novelty products company. 'Course I have to sell to stores and like that, but I'm supposed to try out new stuff on friends and neighbors. Listen, I can give you the wholesale price, how about that!!!"

"Hi, Silvia, uh, we're kind of busy with this important novel…," Joe said.

"Joe! You'd be interested in this one...you work at that cement company ordering parts people pestering you with requests?"

"They sure do, Silvia, why just yesterday....this impatient jerk comes in...'I requested 1000 stainless steel drizzle-snaps with anti-friction drift flanges'...."

"This is it! Just bring out this."

She held out a flat cardboard cutout shaped like a violin. The words "**Sad Story Violin**" in lacy large script was printed on it.

Silvia said, "Here I'll show you. Let me sit behind your desk, I'll pretend to be you, and you be the jerk, OK? Should be easy for you. Now come and ask about the 1000 drift-staffs."

"Drizzle-snaps."

"OK, go ahead." Silvia lounged back and put her feet up on the desk and grabbed a copy of the magazine "Beach Bimbos" from the pile of clutter.

Joe approached and asked, "Silvia, where are those...."

"No, I'm Joe, you're Silvia!"

"Joe, where the Heck are those 1000 drizzle-snaps that...

Silvia(alias Joe) held up her hand. "Wait a sec, let me put a placemark here ..interesting article, an essay on Einstein's Theory of Relativity."

She took out the Sad Story Violin and pretended to play...

"Now what was it you were saying?"

She pressed a button and the electronic chip began to play the somber strains of *"Les larmes de la Mort"* by Allehandro What's His Name.

"Mmm-la-hmm mummum- la-la-de-dah- hmm ...mummum-la-la-de-dah- hmm..."

Or in Modified Austro-Hungarian notation (1795 revised version):
"e↑ ↓d↕e←f→e∂∞a∆g≈e↑d   ↓a↕←g→g∂f∞   f∆a≈e↑f ↓d↕e←a→c∂d ∞f∆e≈a↑d ↓a↕←f→e∂e∞a∆≈c↑ ↓a↕←a→e ∂d∞a∆f≈c↑ ↓↕←f→f∂∞a∆≈d↑ ↓e" (allegro)

"OK, OK, Silvia, ha,ha,ha,..nobody's going to buy this lame gag....."

"But a little humor can lighten up things, deflect ill will."

Sam said, "Silvia, tell you what. I'll buy one of these...the stupid violin thing, if you help with the novel.... here, take a look at the beginning of it, see what you think,...Joe's helping, too"

"Oh, Good Grief, I thought you'd come to your senses and given up by now..."

Silvia plunked down and quickly read. As she ploughed through it she kept mumbling, "Good Grief".

Silvia fidgeted. "Mmmm, what's this about a tablecloth crossword? Do you have one?"

"We were about to draw one up to create a realistic environment to help with the novel , but we were interrupted by a joke saleslady," said Sam.

Silvia thought the crossword was great, much to the surprise of the struggling writers, and she helped make up a complete 15 x15 table-size crossword.

When it was finished, Silvia said, "Great, now just let me borrow this for a bit, I'll bring it back."

"Wait, we need it for the captain's cabin…" But Silvia had already rolled up the paper and whisked it away with her out the door.

"Crazy Silvia. I'll get on with the story, Sam."

Crew members were curious about the crossword novelty, and soon were kibitzing.

"Sir, the men are complaining that they have no interesting crosswords games in the crew's mess."

"Oh Good Grief, Mr. Christian, tell them Tough Beansie!"

Oh, Heck, Sam, this is going nowhere!! Pick another random word.

Sam closed his eyes and stabbed at the dictionary page with his pencil. "Beach ball," he said.

"This is even stupider than the crossword!" But he wrote on:

Puffing on his Meerschaum, First Mate Tulley remarked, "We have that stopover at Bermuda, methinks we best be served iff'n we had us beach balls, and them swim fins, y'know. We got that stuff in the rainy-day locker?"

"Stop. Stop," said Sam as he stabbed again with the pencil. "Diving suit," he called out.

"More like it," Joe said and soon was typing away. Sam went out to get them a pizza and beer. Joe kept going, " tucca, tucca,… ticci, tucca…. tucca, tucca,… ticci, tucca…..."

New characters, Terrence and Looty appeared, and playfully tried on the ship's diving suit and pumped air in with the primitive hand pump. This led to getting the ship's sailmaker to make puffy balloon suits with rubberized canvas- what a great thing to prevent injury from falling. Mocked at first, some of the crew saw their benefits when they thought of high seas that tossed deckhands, knocking them about. Terrence and Looty were unfazed by critics, and made several of the clever air-filled suits. They would be good man-overboard protection, too.

****

A few days later Silvia stopped by Sam's place and Joe was there, too.

"What's this, you're still doing that Novel of the Absurd? Mind if I have some of that pizza, by the way? Thanks."

She munched and read over the latest of the stalled novel. "Balloon suits? Aren't these people supposed to be fighting a war against Spain or somebody? They got time for games?

"Hey, listen, I've got another gag item to sell you. It's Charley Chip."

Charley was a black cardboard computer memory chip about two feet long and a foot wide. Dual inline package, 96-pins, 48 on each side. Fake smile if you ask me.

"See, you come to work in the morning and Charley is sitting in your chair! 'What's going on?' you ask. As you get close a motion detector starts him talking."

"Sorry to tell you, Pal, but you've been replaced by a computer chip...me, Charley Chip, in fact. You probably knew it was coming, Man, it's the computer age. ....Say, would you mind plugging me in, I've been running on batteries, and I'm bushed.

"Silvia this is so dumb. Especially that smirk on Charley's face."

"Hey, Charley, I've got a different job for you. Waste Basket Inspector!" Sam picked up poor Charley and headed for the trash bin.

Charley protested, "Unhand me now, inferior human! Guard! Guard!"

****

A week later. No progress on the exciting sea saga <u>Reggie Danderspoon- Midshipman.</u>

"I think next we should prepare to leave the pier, cast off the strings. You've got two chapters of loading cannonballs and crackers and it's time to get going!"

"Knock, knock, knock." Silvia again. This time she brought two six-packs of beer!

"That's a little thank you for the bubble-suit idea. I'm going to propose it to my boss. See, first sell to places like senior living places where people can fall and break a hip, then maybe young people would want them if they're skateboarding or even biking. They're light and people could just lie down anywhere, take a nap in the park, or when camping

"Silvia, is this one of your jokes? That was just a stupid story gimmick. Nobody is going to put on an air-filled fat-suit!! .You are working for Jokey Joe's...is it one of your jokes?.."

"No, no, no my boss can sell anything, don't forget. And speaking of jokes, you brought it up, didn't you? Here's a winner: "Professor Penelope Parrot!"

It was a stylish green cardboard parrot about two feet high that could perch on your desk or filing cabinet.

"She likes these little crackers, see, she's gotta have a snack when you do."

Silvia stuffed a cracker into Penelope's beak and she said, **"AWWWK, Thanks, Matey. You're doing a good job! AWWWK!"** Penelope said that, not Silvia..

"See? A morale builder, too!"

Silvia went on, "Now I'll pose a typical question that you, Joe, might ask in your fascinating cement company clerk's job:"

"Penelope, Dear, should I order 10 more cloggle-dobbits, so I'll have them on hand?"

Penelope answered, **"AWWWK! Twinkie, did you ask the question: 'Penelope, Dear, should I order 10 more cloggle-dobbits, so I'll have them on hand?' AWWWK?"**

Silvia whispered, "She calls everybody, Twinkie, just say 'Yes' "

Joe said, "Yes"

Penelope said**, "AWWWK! Twinkie, do you think 'Penelope, Dear, should I order 10 more cloggle-dobbits, so I'll have them on hand?' is advisable? AWWK?"**

Joe said, "No"

Penelope said, **"AWWK! Twinkie, my advice is 'Penelope, Dear, should I order 10 more cloggle-dobbits, so I'll have them on hand?' is not advisable at this time, AWWK!"**

"Isn't she great? Fun all the time, only $9.95."

But Joe, still struggling to write more of the novel, said, "Silvia, please get out of here with your stupid parrot!"

Penelope answered, **"AWWWK! Twinkie, did you ask the question: 'Silvia, please get out of here with your stupid parrot!'? AWWWK"**

"YES!"

****

Joe's pencil fell on the word "cookie".

"Oh Good Grief," said Sam, but he started to type. Soon the stalwart crew of HMS IronWood was enjoying regular batches of square sugar cookies. The ship's cook, Cookie, was very busy. Not just any cookies but cookies decorated with letters, complete alphabets that were used to fill in the spaces of the multiple giant crosswords on every tablecloth. And yet still the novel kept grinding to a halt.

Silvia stopped by again. "ALPHABET COOKIES FOR THE CROSSWORDS!" she exclaimed when she read the latest page of the limping narrative, and she rushed out the door.

"Crazy," said Joe. They headed out to get coffee and bagels.

A month went by. The novel pages gathered dust. Joe ordered cement company parts and Sam collected thousands of dishes from Third Avenue Bar tables.

Silvia appeared at Sam's dressed in a very swanky outfit.

"Silvia, you look more beautiful than ever tonight," blurted Sam.

"You're a dear, Sam. I'm on my way to a show with Nicky. But I had to stop by, see, I'm sorry, but your lease will be up in a few days and we have an important tenant who needs more room and he has priority, you know, been here longer,…"

"But Silvia, the Gergens didn't say anything…"

"Well, see, I bought the building from them. Jokey Joe's been selling crosswords and cookies and balloon suits like crazy, so I got a pretty big raise, several times my old salary, no, a hundred times maybe, oh, I don't know, maybe more."

"But listen, I wouldn't want you to leave, there's a swell couple of rooms below street level down by the bowling alley, you get first refusal on it! Bye for now."

****

A week later Sam was sitting in his new flat, B-13. Joe stopped by.

"Sam, what's with this pile of boxes crowding up the place, oh I see, they're those idiot parrots."

"Yes, Silvia's storing them here for awhile, she said they never sold very well. Well, I could have told her that."

"Is this near the bowling alley, Sam?"

Just then there was a sound. "Bonggg...RRRRRRRRRR BOOM BAH BOOMBA BOOOM CADDADDA!!! And the wall shook.

A chorus of Penelopes said, **"AWWWK! ! Twinkie, did you ask the question: 'Bonggg...RRRRRRRRRR BOOM BAH BOOMBA BOOOM CADDADDA!!!'? AWWWK?"**

"AWWWK! ! Twinkie, did you ask the question: 'Bonggg...RRRRRRRRRR BOOM BAH BOOMBA BOOOM CADDADDA!!!'? AWWWK"?

251

"AWWWK! !   Twinkie, did you ask the question: 'Bonggg…RRRRRRRRRR BOOM BAH BOOMBA BOOOM CADDADDA!!!'? AWWWK"?

………………

Iggy Pfaff- Assist. Clerk

OK, I admit it. I hate making phone calls so I wasn't that unhappy went my phone went dead. I don't know why it went dead, unless it was because I'd pulled it off my desk onto the cement floor for the twentieth time. Can I help it if I have to pace back and forth waiting for idiots who put me on hold, so sometimes, you know, the cord isn't that long, and "KLONK! DING!". (I don't know what kind of phone you have, but mine has the old mechanical bell.)

Mr. Boss (not his real name) came by. "Did you make those calls about the rivets and the dustpans and the clevis hooks and the relieving splices and the filler bulbs and the grab snars?"

"Assistant Maintenance Clerk", that's my job title, so I had to do that stuff. If you must know, my Uncle Phil (loading dock veteran) got me the job.

I explained the puzzling phone problem. "I reported it to Maintenance. They should be here soon."

Not too soon, I thought, since I gave them the wrong room number.

Somebody called Mr. Boss away, so he stopped bugging me. I went back to reading my interesting comic, "Sheena, Queen of the Jungle." Where does Sheena get her clothes, anyway? Are there Macy's stores there somewhere in the jungle? Maybe she makes her own, wouldn't take much material, actually. Just because I'm only a clerk, doesn't mean I don't have an inquiring mind.

You could say I'm important enough to have my own office. But you'd also have to say it's the seventh floor utility room with a giant ventilation fan going, and other equipment that involves pipes and valves.

Funny thing about this ventilation system: If I put my ear against the big intake louver, I could overhear conversations. Not that I would do such a sneaky thing, you understand. One of the voices was my very own lovable boss and I sometimes could tell he was about to come give me a stack of chits or invoices or other depressing papers to work on, so I could perhaps escape somewhere or at least look busy.

Of course I was then pretty new at the company, so I didn't recognize some of these disembodied voices.

One morning I craned my neck to listen. My collar and tie chafed. Get rid of this silly tie, I thought. Then I remembered the reason I wore it: To impress Lucy the mail person, the angelic young thing I hoped to see more of, if only she would brush off all the other fellows in the office.

Wonder of wonders, right then Lucy appeared and plunked down a foot-high stack of letters, small packages, bills, and Maintenance Requests.

"Mr. Boss would like you to handle all this right away," she said.

"No trouble at all," says I, as I swept the lot neatly into the waste basket.

"They told me you were a crazy person, you know," she said, squinting her light blue eyes just a bit.

She glanced down. "What's this? Did you draw this?"

"I doodle when I talk on the phone to the hundreds of jerky companies, they put you on hold for hours, you know."

"Listen, don't tell anybody this, but I write children's stories and I'm writing a bee story... I could use illustrations... Can I have this? I'll make a copy and give it back."

I was only half listening, because I was straining to hear through the vent.

"Say, Lucy. I'm sure you would know; whose voice is this?" I put my ear closer to the vent. It was a man's voice that came through pretty loud, kind of Eastern European accent, it seemed.

"That's Mr. Tyrant (not his real name)," she said. "I'm going to report you for eavesdropping, Mr. Snoop!"

Lucy was just kidding around, I hoped.

255

"He showed up a week ago to save the company. Ever hear of 'Chainsaw Al'? His brother, I think."

She lowered her voice. "Don't talk too loud, they probably can hear us, too."

Lucy leaned her svelte self close to the listening vent and waved me over. I bent over to listen, too. Mmmm. How nice indeed, so close to Lucy... what a beautiful name, don't you think? And perfume, or powder, just a bit...

The mumbling through the ducts got louder.

"...Don't do the talk to me 'bout DELETED Cement, those pirates! DELETED! That shugatzin! I croosh like a boog!"

"Do you mean 'Bug', Boss?" somebody said.

We listened a little bit more. I guessed the new top man was not a softy. Then a new voice, soft and feminine: "Mr. Ty(not his real nickname), are you ready to dictate the letter?"

Lucy stood up. "Oh my Gawd! I can't listen anymore. That's Big Wiggie's secretary, Ms. Icicle (not her real name). Did you see her David Ochlessey outfit yesterday? If you can't afford Ochlessey, you buy Prada, you know? Did she rob a bank? I gotta go."

I sat still, reliving the recent minutes. Lucy, the real Lucy, darling of the office, actually was here talking to me, more or less, for seven minutes!

My reverie was rudely interrupted when the door of my private office (utility room) flew open with a bang.

A gorilla came in and frowned at me.

He called to his buddy. "Hey Rocco, they lied to us, this room's got furniture and a guy."

Construction work was underway in Biggie's office. Upshot: about a hundred boxes of files got dumped in my cramped room.

The next day I was trying to re-box a thousand snap-gullets. Somebody ordered the wrong size (OK, me) and I had to send them back, but I dropped them and they started rolling all over the place. "@#%&^^$*," I said to them.

Just then I heard a soft sweet voice. I recognized it, it was Ms. Icicle, and as I gaped up at her perfect face, her perfect figure, her perfect David Ochlessey attire, her light brown hair falling lightly upon her azure silk scarf, she said, "My Dear Insect, are you Iggy Pfaff?" No, all right, actually it was, "Are you Iggy Pfaff?"

As I stammered, she explained a problem. In the construction turmoil some very important personal papers of hers had gotten mixed up with the multitudinous files that were now glutting my meager quarters.

Would I help her find them? Would I? Would I like to spend some time with a twenty-one-year-old absolute knockout, a very healthy one? Yes, yes, yes!

But it turned out the way for me to help was to stay out of my office/utility room for two days while she had two junior suits rifle files until the papers turned up. OK. That's my lot in life.

Not quite the end of the matter, however.

The next day, she returned, and sat on a file box and gave a frustrated little sigh. She even referred to the two afore-mentioned suits as "two dumb lackeys". She was still missing some pages.

"Izzy…"

"It's 'Iggy'," I corrected.

"Iggy, Mr. Ty is usually nice to me, but this is really not company stuff, you know, it's my own that I worked on at lunchtime… a children's story. Those dodos only found part of my originals, there are seven pages more. I can't look myself, my boss keeps me busy all the time…Oops, my beeper, gotta go."

I agreed to find them, of course.

****

What a break! I found them right away, since they had apparently dropped out of a folder onto the floor under my ratty desk. I called Ms. I. and left a voice-mail: "Missing papers found."

It was a mouse story and the start of a bee story. Reggie Mouse…dreams of being a pilot…why doesn't he dream of being a cheese thief, anyway? Got a chance there.

More phone calls, I doodled as usual. Mice appeared on my

scraps of paper.

"Look, I just want the plexis flenders, standard radius of 18 mm. Is it so hard? Do you have to put me on hold?"

I drew bees. What do they look like anyway? How do they fly, the little Fatties?

Then the Executive Secretary greatly admired by me, disparaged as Ms. Icicle in some quarters, but whose actual name was Wanda, returned, entering hurriedly.

"Izzy, I'm glad you're still here, ...oh Gosh, you found them! I could kiss you!"

"OK by me," I didn't say. Wanda was smiling. Fortuna was smiling.

"I see you've been drawing....... why, those bees are just WONDERFUL ...and really cute mice!"

Her dreamy eyes expressed wonder looking at me. Her eyes said, "Could this bush-league sack of potatoes actually produce drawings??"

"Izzy."

"Iggy."

"Iggy, your bees are perfect for a children's book, really, they have depth of character, the kind of bee you want to be friends with and ...say, it's late and I have to meet a girl friend. Iggy, maybe we could work together on some stories..."

Naturally, I was frozen into immobility and disbelief...I commanded my face to smile and say yes, yes, yes, but no sound came out.

"Of course, I know you must be very busy with the........ maintenance things."

"NOO! NO! NO! not busy, are you kidding?" my brain said, but she only saw my catatonic stare.

"We'll talk, Iggy." And she was gone. Door shut.

"YES, I'D LOVE TO, WANDA!" I said to the empty room.

About ten seconds went by.

The door opened again. Lucy breezed in. "Well, what did the princess want? I saw her come in here."

"Big Boss sent her to check on the boxes, I guess. She took some stuff."

"Say, Iggy, you're doing mouse drawings? You know, I'm doing a mouse story, too."

Unfortunately, my idiot boss barged in and barked at me to get moving pronto to Building Seven to get some Sperry clasps or Berry hasps or something so I got going before he could give me a Mr. Dithers style prompting.

I don't mind telling you that it was a frustrating trip. They gave me the run-around and I had to go to Building Twelve...I was sweating and dragging when I got back with the Kerry rasps.

No Lucy by the time I got back. It was after quitting time. But guess what, Lucy had left notes about a whole bunch of bumble bee illustrations to continue the story. Little hearts appeared floating above my head. I'll do dozens of sketches for her, we'll have lunch together... Wait, there is a cloud...if she finds out I'm helping her big rival, Wanda, what then?

The door opened again. It was Beefy, an old pal. Nice guy, Beefy, works down on the mixing floor and had a tell-tale coat of lime dust.

"Iggface! I saw a gorgeous daffodil coming out of your room here. Must be some mistake, eh?"

"Potentially great for me, but I'm worried sick, Beefy. I'll tell you while we have a beer at the Third Street Bar."

We made our way two blocks to the bar. The bartender, Jake, greeted us and set us up.

I explained more to my friend. Maybe he'll have some ideas. But wise guy Beefy now says, "So what's your problem? I can picture a New York Post headline: 'QUALITY CHICKS ACT-UALLY TALK TO MAINTENANCE DRONE!'."

"Oh, ha, ha," I said.

"Jake, this guy is getting some attention from TWO, count 'em, TWO hotties, and he's frowning!"

I explained the whole deal to Jake, too. Lucy is writing children's stories, Wanda is writing children's stories, somehow both saw bee sketches I was doodling. OK, so far, but Lucy hates Wanda, so if she finds out I even talked to Wanda, she'll never speak to me, probably. And vice versa would not surprise me.

Jake: "My advice is pick one; two-timing never works. Second advice: secrets around the office last as long as soap bubbles in a desert."

****

Then and later I thought and thought. Yes, I would simply make excuses to Wanda...gulp...be a little too busy...and turn into a bee-drawing fool for the dear and angelic Lucy!

I slept fitfully and sat up at 2:30 AM. Just one change, I thought: It's Lucy I'll put off, "Just can't seem to get these bees right, Lucy."...."Boy, Bossman just doesn't give me time for mice or bees"...and precious, regal Wanda, Wanda, Wanda! As many bees, mice, as you want in my best artistic (doodling) style!

Then I slept in peace. Grabbed a coffee on my way to work. Passed through the office. Lucy was at her desk . She brushed her hair back with three fingers, then held her hand in midair the way she does and ...just one thing, just one thing, I said inside my head, it's the aloof Wanda I will ever so politely not help...it's Lucy, Lucy of the golden hair, Lucy, girl of my dreams whom I will shower with every drawing within my power.. Yes. Lucy.

****

My phone was ringing as I came into my rather crowded utility office.

It was Wanda: "Your drawings are great Iggy. Could you change a couple, to have the papa bee talking on the phone?"

"Yes, of course, no problem," I heard myself saying. What Wanda wants, Wanda gets. I dropped all the silly company papers and drew several sketches. They looked pretty much like bees, too, good enough for a little kid. What do they know?

I also worked a lot in the afternoon on Lucy drawings, between phone calls. Well, one phone call. My boss was out and it was quiet.

I called Lucy. "It's Iggy, Lucy…"

"Yes, who again? Are you the Xerox guy? Listen that machine is… oh, Iggy, Utility Room Iggy.

"Oh sure, I'll stop by at break time, thanks so much for drawing these, I can't wait to see them."

She's a sweetheart, Lucy. She came by and admired everything.

"Yes, I admit I was a little surprised. I thought you were, well, kind of a drudge. Ha, ha, I was wrong… I thought you just did your extremely boring job with hardware invoices and all that and just went to some joint like the Third Street Bar after work and talked to the bartender or something. Ha, ha."

"Ha, ha, ha," I agreed, stretching my collar a bit.

Lucy made some notes, and pasted some page roughs. I

leaned close to inhale her femme fatale perfume. Ahhhh.

Phone rings. It's Wanda, but I pretend it's some company jerk.

She asks for a bee with a typewriter scene, not a bee talking on a phone. I answer like I'm in a spy movie, "Oh yes, the type of wire we use, yes, #88, OK."

Wanda's voice over the phone: "What???...Oh, I see, somebody's there... who?"

I continue in a bored voice, "It's Lu...Luke who sometimes stops by to pick up clips or spring rivets, stuff like that. Yes, I got it about the type of wire, Fred, see ya."

"Fred? That sounded like a woman's voice from here," Lucy said.

"The phone lines have a funny effect, don't they?"

Just then Beefy came in, only a little dusty today.

"Say, Iggy, I wanted to show you something, when you have a minute. Hi, Lucy."

The big vent fan kicked off just then as it often does and the sound of voices filtered faintly from the louver.

I could hear faint voices through the ducts, one of them was Wanda in her melodious tone, "Mr. Ty, I've got to go get some files from the utility room, be back in a jiffy." "Yeah, sure," says Bigwig.

Oh, oh, I'm in trouble.

"Maybe we should finish this later, Lucy, I just remembered I've got to load some toggles right away, Building Nine."

I got up and went to the door. "Thought I heard somebody calling for you, Lucy…maybe you'd better scoop up all that and….I can help you."

"Oh, sure, I'm almost done with this, pretty neat story flow, if I do say so. See the surprise on the last page?"

That wasn't the only surprise.

My door opened and the Ice Princess herself came in and we all peered silently for a moment at Lucy's story paste-up.

Wanda said, looking at me, "Well."

"It certainly looks like Ms. Lucille Naismith is composing a story using drawings which Mr. Ignatius Pfaff drew for a story of mine, namely: 'Billy Bee Goes to School'."

"What would you say to that?" she said, looking at me.

"Gulp," I gulped.

Lucy looked up slowly. "Iggy has been helping you write a story, Wanda? Is it about the North Pole?" she asked in a frosty tone.

"Ladies, I must point out that the bees are not the same bees, you know, I would never do that."

"They look exactly the same to me," said Wanda.

"Well," Said Lucy.

"I'm not happy, Lucy," said Wanda.

"I'm not happy, Wanda," said Lucy.

For awhile it was all quiet on the Western Front. Wanda scowled at the paste-up.

Beefy shifted on his feet. "Ummm, I can see you're busy, Iggy. I'll stop by another time…"

Wanda leaned slightly to look at Lucy's story rough: "Is that supposed to be a surprise ending, Lucy?"

"Wanda, careful, or you'll get ink on Mr. Ralph's scarf."

Wanda leaned over and whispered to Lucy, "mmmp…..hmm …hmmigh…mmmhph."

"Filene's!??? Really? Ha, ha, ha."

Much merriment over this. Can you understand women?

More whispers, and gestures.

"Not Penney's??!! Ha,ha,ha,ha,"

"Hey, listen, Lucy, feel this fabric, and…. mmmmmdfrg… whmmmm…. hmmm."

"Wait, you'll love this, from Helen in Purchasing….mmmmph mmmph… mmnmh…nmmmth"

"Wanda, one thing: mmmph…mmnmh…nmmmth."

"Beefy, what was it you wanted to show me?" I asked.

He flipped open a manila folder.

"I know you were doing bee drawings. Here's another way. See? I took these photos and just did a little Photoshop touch-up."

The girls craned their necks to see. Lucy was really enthused.

"WOW! What a great effect! Look at that, Wanda!" she said.

This was outdone by Wanda. "Really, really outstanding, for sure! You did these? What was your name, again?"

"They call me Beefy," said Beefy, modestly.

Wanda exclaimed some more: "Lucy, these photos jump out at you, the characters come alive, right out of the page!"

"Beefy, I love the little table and typewriter! How did you do that?"

"It's just made from matchboxes and paperclips and things, …in an appropriate size, you know."

My former friend, Beefy, continued, "These can also be done in 3-D, and printed right on the page with a lenticular process. I can show you that tomorrow, if you want."

A beeper went off.

Wanda said, "Mr Ty. I gotta go now."

"Just quickly, Wanda… mmmmmhp…. mnhgh… mnnhg," whispered Lucy.

"Oh, really?

"Yes, she's a new agent, but very active, loves this genre."

"Listen, we'll have lunch and we'll talk, OK?"

"Sure, Third Street Bar is good…"

Wanda: "Listen,…uhh, Beefy. Can you be at the Third Street Bar at 12 noon tomorrow? And bring all your stuff?"

Beefy stammered, "Be glad to. Uh, I gotta go now, cement to make."

"Me, too, Guys," said Lucy.

"See ya, Iggy."

"See ya, Iggy."

"See ya, Iggy."

Show Business

Wanna get into Show Business? You gotta pay your dues, Man. That's why I answered that ad for a Theatrical Director. It wasn't Broadway. Actually, it was DELETED State Prison. Dish-washing wasn't getting me very far, so what the Heck.

I made my way past the barbed wire and guards to the Warden's Office. Wow, the warden looked so familiar, but I couldn't place him. I knew I'd seen that face somewhere.

"Governor's wife dreamed up this stupid fiasco," he said. "You were the only applicant, so you've got the job," he continued, through his cigar smoke.

"Thank, you, Sir. If I may suggest a theatrical work to start things off, it happens that I wrote a play, "Lollipop Parade", a lighthearted....."

"Mizz Gov calls the shots, Buddy. Here's your play. Get going on it. I'll round up some warm bodies to be your actors." He tossed over a script. It was a ballet: "Flowers of Summer". As I was leaving, I remembered where I'd seen that face: Mr. Potato Head.

I was given an actual office! It was in the boiler room, but it was a roomy enough, except for the boilers and pumps. It didn't have any windows, but it did have a lot of steam valves and pipes running around the room which would be great if it ever got cold in (warm state), like during the next Ice Age. The furnishings were on the practical side, consisting of a wooden crate for a desk and a tar bucket to sit on.

But don't think I wasn't important. I was assigned a Personal Secretary. His name was Gizzard Smith and he was an artist doing time for assault with a deadly pair of scissors; apparently somebody had criticized his painting. I wasn't sure I wanted a secretary, especially one with a nasty temper. And now I would have to request another crate and tar bucket for him.

Now, don't get the idea that Gizz wasn't a fun guy. The next day I returned to find he had painted all the walls to look like a WW II submarine control room.

"What do you think of my painting?" he asked, beaming.

"Wonderful!" I said.

"See, here's your periscope," he explained. "Look in here."

He had stuck a cardboard eyepiece onto one of the large vertical pipes. I looked into it and could see little ship silhouettes painted on the horizon, and a little paper moon above a cardboard sea.

"Captain," said Gizzard, "there's a ship closing in on us."

"What?" I said. "Now wait a minute, Gizzard, I don't want to play submarine."

"Captain, Sonar reports an enemy tin can on our tail," Gizzard went on, "should we rig for silent running and rest her on the bottom?"

I paused.

"Captain, shall we take her to the bottom?" he asked, more urgently.

"It's too deep, Mr. Smith," I replied evenly. "This baby would crack like an eggshell. We'll have to turn and fire our last two fish right down their throats."

I checked my instrument panel.

"Hard right rudder. Hold her steady at fifty feet," I coolly commanded. "Call the Torpedo Room and have them set those fish for one thousand yards."

"One thousand yards? But, Sir, we'll be too close," said my timid Executive Officer.

"You heard the order, Mr. Smith," I said sternly. "Up periscope."

I leaned over and peered through the glass- we were so close I could see those grinning enemy sailors on the bow.

"Stand by to fire One and Two," I said.

"Stand by to fire One and Two, Aye," came the reply.

"Fire One! Fire Two!"

"I'LL FIRE YOU, YOU NITWIT!" said the warden, who had come in without even knocking. "What the $%#&%$& are you doing?"

Fine, Warden, I thought to myself. See if we ever let you play.

After he had calmed down, the warden told me that he had assembled twenty men to be the new theater company. He had an interesting auditioning method: he picked names beginning with "A" through "G".

"Got to get going on this, Mizz Gov expects to see this in two weeks. Your cast is down in the exercise room now, get 'em going on it."

A short time later, in the exercise room, I gave a short rundown of the plan. Performance in two weeks, rehearsals every day. Silent stares from my players.

"Excuse me, Sir. I've had some theater experience, maybe I could take one of the lead roles?" offered Stoneface. "Who is the main character?"

"All the characters are important. I suppose the cricket is kind of a leading one."

"A cricket? Who are the other characters?"

"Well, there are quite a number of flowers, and a ladybug."

"Sir, I got an idea," said Bones. "How about we do 'The Caine Mutiny' or maybe 'Death of a Salesman'? "

"Nope, warden gave me this," I said.

Mug piped up: "You know, Sir, most of the guys don't want to be no flowers. Instead of flowers and crickets, how about we can be <u>ants</u>. That's almost the same as crickets. Then we could do a real good play called 'The War of the Ants'... black against the red..."

"Yeah!" said somebody.

"That's good- 'War of the Ants'," said another mutineer.

"I'm sorry," I said firmly. "We only have a script for 'Flowers of Summer'."

"Just change it a little," continued Mug. "OK, picture this: Scene I: We see the good guy black ants- they're vegetarians- don't kill nobody. They have nice nurse ants to take care of their cute little larvae grubs... they are social insects, always invite friends over to play cards, you know, and generally they like to drink beer, go bowling. Nice fun guys.

"But now Scene II shows the red, bloodsucking, Communist ants... they eat other insects with their vicious big jaws. They keep aphids for milk and kick them. They have soldier ants who march around with a goose step. And instead of a queen ant, they have a ruthless tyrant ant!

"Then, in Act II, a merciless attack by the red ants almost destroys the poor black ant colony. They kill a lot and take prisoners. But slowly the wounded black ants start to recover. They call some of their buddies who are National Guard army ants, and they all go to the red ant colony…"

"Luckily, the red ants have all gorged themselves and gotten drunk on honey wine, the slobs, so the gentle black ants are victorious… the red ant colony is destroyed and they are driven from the land; plus the black ants get their TV sets and stuff!"

This brought cheers of approval from the crowd.

"Well, perhaps that would add some drama to 'Flowers of Summer'," I admitted.

"Yes Sir, and I'm sure we could write that script with your help, what with your knowledge of the theater and all," said Mug.

"Well, yes, maybe with my help."

On Friday morning, using my square Bakelite phone, I called the warden to discuss getting some costumes.

Ms. Bullard, his secretary, who had all the charm of a rusty muffler, informed me that any questions I had should be directed to my immediate supervisor.

"Who is my immediate supervisor?" I asked innocently.

As a matter of fact, it had been left to her to place me in the big friendly prison bureaucracy, and she had stuck me in the lowest possible position, namely, working for Mr. Sedgwick, the Purchasing Clerk.

She also explained an important principle of the prison procedures, and that was: don't ever call her again.

It was warm in my boiler room office. I loosened my tie and began reading Staging Musicals.

I was pleasantly surprised when a very beautiful ballerina dressed in white appeared at my office and beckoned me to follow her. I found that I could dance as effortlessly as she... she spun away like a white veil in the wind... I followed... floating to her side with one gazelle-leap. She pirouetted into my arms and moved her lips toward mine and whispered:

"WAKE UP, YOU BIMBO!"

The ballerina had turned into Mr. Sedgwick.

"I was not asleep," I explained. "I just had my head close to the book because I am nearsighted."

With his characteristic rudeness, Mr. Sedgwick introduced me to Mr. Ross from the State Cultural Office and left. Also present was a tall man holding his head tipped away from the steam pipes.

"The governor's wife wants to spare no expense to ensure the success of your theater program," said Mr. Ross. "Mr. DELETED, here, is in this country on an exchange program. He is a stage set designer who is renowned all over his native country, DELETED.

It was further explained that I had but to make known my requirements and the finest sets would be provided plus all costumes as well.

"I was thinking of maybe a big anthill with multiple openings and passageways," I suggested. "What do you think, Mr. DELETED?"

"Raibilli ahm naboliox tajkab grituko abba, clabi?" said Mr. DELETED.

"Oh, I forgot to mention that Mr. DELETED does not speak English, but I can interpret for him," said Mr. Ross.

Now our foreign friend brought out a portfolio to show me. It consisted of many photographs of people holding their mouths open, showing quite a few cavities and dental problems and how they were fixed.

"Why is he showing me pictures of teeth?" I asked. "Our play is not about teeth," I assured him.

Mr. Ross spoke directly to his friend.

"Whya teethy? What Hella fora?" asked Mr. Ross, in the native language of DELETED.

Some further discussion and gesturing ensued. It seemed Mr. DELETED was actually a dentist and did not want to build our stage sets for us, even though the dental business was slow, what with everybody using Crest these days.

Nonplussed only briefly, Mr. Ross returned the next day with a real stage designer from DELETED, whose native language Mr. Ross spoke as fluently as that of DELETED. Scenery and costumes were to be forthcoming in time for the opening.

Rehearsals were going OK. One afternoon we were treated to a great spoof of the warden by Drumstick, complete with giant ears, and exaggerated Hitler uniform, etc. We all were having a hearty laugh, except for one figure at the back of the darkened room. That was the warden, who was sitting in on the rehearsal.

You know how people talk about getting a "pink slip"… which means they are fired? I found out they aren't always pink. The one I got was white.

I went back to my desk (crate) to get my pencils, comics, and big-eared voodoo doll and left. I even remembered to turn off the lights as I went out. In fact I turned off all the steam valves that were handy, too.

I plodded back to town. Where would I go? Chicago. I went to the bus depot/drug store to get a ticket. The very attractive girl in front of me bought a ticket to Los Angeles, where she would seek her fortune in show business, she told the clerk.

Suddenly, I had an idea. Maybe I would go to Los Angeles, then go to Chicago some other time.

"Now that's a coincidence!" I said casually. "I'm going to L.A., too."

"Really?" asked Blue Eyes. "Are you in show business?"

"Well, as a matter of fact, I am…"

Presently the bus pulled up and my lovely new acquaintance got on. I was just boarding when a large hairy hand clamped on my shoulder.

"There's been a change in plans," said the warden. "We need you back at the prison."

It is best not to argue with someone who has vise-grips for fingers, so I went with him. On the drive back to DELETED Prison, he explained that he had forgotten that in the general scheme of things, governor's wives can kick wardens out into the street any day of the week, even if said wardens are only two and half years away from retirement.

Back at the Castle, I found my desk and antique phone set up in the corridor, which I took to be a subtle hint that I was not completely reinstated.

Stoneface was coming along well in the part of the red queen, but unfortunately he got paroled. I asked if he would like to stay another month to help us out but he declined, since he was kind of looking forward to getting the &^%^%$% out of &^%%$%% DELETED Prison.

I did not want my ants to be without a queen, so I stepped in to play this important role myself. At the time I was about eighty pounds overweight, so I was well suited to play a queen carrying 200,000 eggs in her abdomen.

We were doing a dress rehearsal one afternoon when a goateed visitor with a funny necktie was ushered over to me. He shook my pincer and introduced himself as Pierre Roquefort, of the Theatre de Art de Paris.

"Monsieur Carlyle, I admire you very much," he said.

"I admire you very much, too," I replied, not wishing to be

outdone. "I particularly like your tie."

"Monsieur, I know you by reputation... and I have seen your work... all excellent. I am here to offer you the position of Master of Theater Arts at our L'Ecole de Theatre Nationale."

"Thank you, I'll take it. When do I start?"

"I am delighted... here is my card. Call me next week."

Things were looking up.

"I presume you saw our rehearsal of 'The War of the Ants'?"

"Alas... I regret that I did not. But I have seen many of your productions... 'Dance of the Rats'... 'Parade of the Insane Teddy Bears'... 'The Busted Music Box'," he said.

"Wait, wait... I think maybe you have the wrong Michael Carlyle."

"Mon Dieu!" You are not the same Michael Carlyle who received the Golden Footlight Award for 'The Flight of the Dodo Birds'?"

"Must be somebody else."

"Haa, ha, ha...," he said as he snatched back his card. "I guess the joke's on me."

"Does that mean I don't get the job?"

"Oui, you don't get the job."

"Monsieur Camembert, you are wearing an extremely ugly tie," I remarked.

On the day of our big performance at the Governor's Mansion, I put on extra deodorant and suited up in my queen ant outfit. I rode in the cab of the flatbed truck carrying our big anthill and the other props. The rest of the prisoner-ants would follow in the van as soon as they were dressed and ready.

A funny thing happened a few miles down the road when we stopped for a red light. I looked back to see <u>nineteen giant ants swarm out of the anthill,</u> and leap and fall off the truck and dash into the woods as fast as their six legs would carry them! Those rascals had played a game of Trojan Anthill on us!

I jumped out of the truck and ran after them.

"Hey guys, come back! What will the warden say? You're going to get me into big trouble!"

After a few minutes I stopped to catch my breath and because I realized I had no way to capture nineteen desperate criminals, even if I did catch up to them. So I went in the opposite direction, toward the truck.

But the truck was nowhere to be seen. I couldn't find the road, either.

Of course I wasn't lost, since I could easily get my bearings from observing moss on the bark of trees- it always grows on the north or ...was it south side or... Let's see, the sun rises in the East, unless you're in Australia. Wouldn't that moss grow on the east side??

But, none of the blasted trees had any moss, anyway. I tried to remember woods lore from those Shredded Wheat boxes. That just made me hungry. If I starved to death, would somebody eventually find my skeleton? Would they notice how many cavities I had? (Note to readers: Remember to brush often and you won't have this worry.)

Now I spied a glimmer of house lights. I was saved! Soon I came out on a road and there it was: "Uncle Bill's Bar and Grill"!

Inside, I ordered a beer and sat down wearily at the bar to drink it. I ignored the yokels who had never seen a giant ant come into a bar for a drink.

The news was on TV over the bar:

"Nineteen dangerous criminals staged a daring escape this afternoon from DELETED Prison. These men are still at large. When last seen they were wearing ant suits. It is speculated that they are all members of a bizarre satanic cult who want insects to control the world."

Just then the bartender brought out his shiny new shotgun to show me, though I hadn't asked to see it.

"That's a beauty," I said amiably.

"Don't-move-one-$&%#$*-inch, Spiderman!" he snapped.

With my four arms in handcuffs I was soon delivered to the prison gate by sheriff's deputies. The warden came out and had a few words with the fuzz. They talked, nodding and pointing at me, which wasn't polite.

An hour later, I was sitting on my suitcase, which had been carefully stuffed with all my belongings, courtesy of the DELETED Sheriff's Department, next to a sign which read:

"YOU ARE NOW LEAVING DELETED COUNTY. Y'ALL COME AGAIN, NOW"

Perhaps it was time for me to move on to other things, I thought. After all, I got the Theater Program firmly established at the prison- that was the hard part- others could carry on.

It was a warm night, and I found some comfortable hay to lie down on. Tomorrow I would hitchhike to Los Angeles and probably meet that girl again. And after all, I got a swell ant suit out of the deal, for free.

I was a weary and bedraggled insect. My eyelids and antennae were drooping and I soon fell asleep.

Library Cats

"Mom, I have to write a story for school tomorrow. Ms. Beasley says we can get help to write the words but it has to be our story that we made up."

"Billy can help you. I'm working on these tax returns," said Mom.

"But Mom, I want to play baseball with Mickey outside."

"After you help your little sister."

"Awww, Mom!" said Billy.

 Billy is eight and writes and spells pretty well.

"I'll tell you the words and you write it down for me, OK, Billy?"

"OK, OK, let's hurry up with your stupid, boring story, I want to go outside and play ball with Mickey."

"Start this way," said Kathy. "Ms. Abigail Francis was the beautiful new librarian at the Smithville Public Library. "

Billy wrote: *"Abbie Freaky was an old bag and got a new job-Slimeville Town Librarian."*

"Did you write the first sentence?"

"Yep, I wrote it. Now what?"

Kathy continued: "She loved her new job and kept all the books in good order and everything was very neat and she was friendly with all the library patrons."

Billy wrote: *"She wore U.S. Army combat boots and smoked cigarettes and left all the books on the floor."*

Kathy continued: "She also loved cats and each day she would bring her cat Furball with her and Furball would sit on the counter and watch as people checked out the books."

Billy wrote: *"The grouchy old woman had a big bulldog who growled and scared the customers."*

Kathy said: "Ms. Harper said it wasn't proper to have a cat in the library as it might get cat fur on the books. It was against town rules."

Billy wrote: *"Two big troopers came in and handcuffed Ms. Freaky and slapped her in jail for violating a town ordinance."*

Kathy said: "A patron told about her friend who was very sad, and Ms. Francis said why not take Furball when you visit to cheer her up."

Billy wrote: *"The town manager heard about the arrest and he came to the jail to fire her from the library job."*

Kathy said: "That made the friend very happy, and so she started to loan out cats because she had several."

Billy wrote: *"Grizzly, the bulldog, went tearing around the library chewing up thousands of books. The place was a shambles."*

Kathy said: "She loaned them out to anyone who was sad or lonely, just like library books, and had a library card for each one."

Billy wrote: *"The town presented Ms. Freaky with a bill for $150,000 for damages."*

Kathy said: "Then the townspeople could see what a good thing it was and they let her have as many cats in the library as she wanted!"

Billy wrote: *"Ms. Freaky's boyfriend, Clyde, helped her break out of jail (a felony) and they escaped in a stolen car."*

Kathy said: "Not only that, but children loved to come to the library to pet the cats and many more came to borrow books than before."

Billy wrote: *"Abbie and Clyde took to robbing stores and soon were wanted in six states."*

Kathy said: "Ms. Francis was delighted when she was given a special award by the local school for encouraging reading!"

Billy wrote: *"Both Abbie and Clyde were arrested after a high-speed chase in Las Vegas and are now serving hard time in San Quentin State Prison."*

"Is it done?" asked Kathy. "Thanks, Billy."

"No problem."

"Now I can pass it in to Ms. Beasley. I'll bet she'll like it."

"I'm sure she will, Kathy. It's not as boring as I thought."

Library Days

One Wednesday, old grumpy Ms. Schnozzletwittle, my boss at the library, (OK, not really her name), was explaining some dumb plan about lining up books on the shelves. She didn't like my way of putting them in order by height. So we had to go by a method preferred by a former governor of New York, which he named after himself and forced libraries to use.

I was trying to sort books according to the crazy system when suddenly a sweet voice said, "Izzy! What are you doing here?" It was the gorgeous sweetheart of the Building 20 Office at the old cement company that had once made the mistake of employing me.

"Lucy! It's great to see you. It's Iggy, by the way."

"Iggy, you know, I have to talk to you about those drawings of bees and mice. I couldn't use Beefy's stuff, it turns out. My publisher turned up her nose and wanted your drawings, but you were gone, by then."

Could this good news really be happening? She of the blue eyes and bright smile actually talking to me again?

I took a break from my exciting library work and we sat and talked over coffee at Betty's Café.

"Iggy, listen, you know, I'm a Gypsy. I kind of believe the fortune tellers, because they are right sometimes, aren't they?"

"Lucy, it is all bunk!" I said.

"Madame Giselle just yesterday read my palm and said I would meet a young man with a scar over his right eye, green eyes and a name beginning with 'P', and he would be my dream come true.

"That's you, Iggy! You have a scar over your right eye and have green eyes and your last name begins with a 'P'!"

"Bunk, but a very logical and true kind of bunk!" I continued.

"Now, Iggy, don't take offense, but when I first met you, you seemed like a first class dork, with points off because you looked like Don Knotts."

"And now?"

"A dork who looks like Don Knotts who can draw bees," she said. "I've got to go. I'll drop by again."

****

The next day I went myself to get a reading from this Madame

Giselle. She said I was a hopeless nerd, so no romance in my future. This I interpreted to mean that I would meet a wonderful young girl named Lucy, who happened to be a Gypsy, and we would soon be happily married. I casually mentioned this result to Lucy.

Lucy did not seem so happy about the all-powerful FATE's arrangements for her, but didn't actually cry. I counted that in my favor.

I discreetly tried to find out more about Madame Giselle. Could she be bribed? After all, a few more words from Madame, and I would be ready to sell my car to buy an engagement ring.

Of course, I wouldn't do such an underhanded, sneaky thing as that. Shame on me.

Madame could contact Lucy and say there was an addendum to her recent reading: "Hurry, a hasty marriage is strongly advised. Don't wait or the opportunity will pass and your only other choice will be an ex-con with no teeth and gray hair."

I would say, "Madame, just this one little favor, here's my IOU for $1,000, what do you say? I'm a Gypsy, too, born in a wagon, you know."

I looked in a mirror. Instead of my usual sunny, handsome, smiling self, I saw a person with a Dorian Gray evil smirk. I decided not to look in mirrors anymore.

****

"Card catalog's over there, Buddy," I really wanted to say, but instead I dug up info about some obscure Neanderthal cave paintings. I was a low-level underling clerk at the library, I guess I was supposed to help.

The goofy-looking fellow wouldn't go away, kept blabbing on about how he was writing this story- a lame tale of a social misfit who moons over a very cute chick, Dee Dee. He helps her fix a radio and she reluctantly rides in his sub-nerd little tin car. They discover the secret workshop of the science teacher who is building a <u>six-legged vehicle that walks like an ant</u>! It's based on prehistoric cave paintings depicting ant-vehicles.

Well, I felt sorry for the poor guy and tried to give some advice. "Lose the ant-car, make it an anti-gravity machine, that's more believable," I said. I don't know if he changed it or not. Of course, nobody would publish his stupid story, anyway.

But I got interested in the details of the supposed ant-vehicles. Hard to believe these cave people built any vehicles, but maybe they could be built now that MIG welding has come in.

I hired Saphead, a garage mechanic friend who was good at welding to help me. We just used a good-sized motorcycle engine, and the rest was just a bunch of links to long legs that moved in a kind of circular motion.

We used steel, not Neanderthal materials like wood and animal skins, that's all. Now I made mine a two-passenger, and let me tell you, it would move! Rev that Harley and claw dirt, Baby! 'Course I had no registration, so had to be discreet about highway use.

****

Lucy appeared again at the library. She leaned just a bit close to me and of course I was in love with her.

"Listen, I've temporarily put aside those children's stories anyway, while I do some magazine articles about oddball societies. It's so unbelievable, really idiot people, some of them!

"Dumb things! Like the Zero Personalities Anonymous! The ZPA. Real losers go to meetings and try to get a life! Ha, ha, ha. It really exists, it's not a joke!"

"Ha, ha, ha," I chuckled.

She looked at me for a moment.

"Actually, Izzy...."

"Iggy."

"Actually, Iggy, now that I think about it, you might want to join- move off square zero. Get so you can say more than 'Oh, I don't know.' in conversation. What do you think?"

"Oh, I don't know," I said.

"The fact is, there is a chapter right here in DELETED."

Lucy looked into my eyes and I was helpless. Wednesday night I went to the local ZPA meeting.

****

The leader was this Mr. Cheerful, who could give Dale Carnegie false enthusiasm lessons. He had on a big beanie with "LOSER" embroidered on it.

"You've taken the first step, LOSERS! You came to this ZPA meeting! See this LOSER hat? I once wore this, but I got rid of it! Like this!"

He struck a match and lit the hat and tossed it into the Permanent Extinction Incinerator, or PEI, or as I would call it, a galvanized ash can.

"Now I can wear any hat I want!"

Then he handed out LOSER beanies to all of us. Kind of a nice beanie, actually, I wanted to keep mine, but no, we all had to parade to the front and toss them into the PEI, which burned them to ashes, and smoked the room more than somewhat.

My eyes watered, but I remembered my promise to Dear Lucy and didn't leave. Mr. Cheerful continued with more pep talk drivel and other folderol. One part was the "Deck of Fate", playing cards with pictures. Each was a personality we had to try for a week, until the next ZPA meeting.

I drew the "Wyatt Earp" card. I had to assume the personality of the famed Western marshal. No problem for Iggy, I thought. I went to a costume shop. They did not have a Wyatt Earp costume, in fact had a pitiful Western selection. I avoided the simpy Roy Rogers fringed number and settled for the Jesse James, which at least had a vest, boots, and nice Stetson-style hat. The cap pistol with it would never do, though, especially with the "Hopalong Cassidy" name on the barrel.

Gun shop was my next stop. They had a used .44 caliber revolver with a six-inch barrel. More like it, Tex!

Of course, being always a law-abiding citizen, more or less, I applied for a permit to carry such a handgun. Bunch of questions on the form. One was: "Reason applicant wishes to carry a handgun."

I answered: "To pretend to be Wyatt Earp".

Mr. Official Clerk voiced some skepticism.

"If you are acting in a play, Sir, why can't you use a stage gun?"

I changed my reason to: "To maintain law and order at my place of employment, the DELETED Public Library."

"Are there valuable books at this library, Sir, requiring armed guard protection?"

"I regard all knowledge to be priceless, Sir."

I ended up with a permit to carry the gun, but not to buy bullets. A fine how-do-you-do, but that's bureaucracy for you.

What's a shootin' iron without bullets, or slugs, as we say out West?

As I was returning to my rooming house, I happened to see a deputy sheriff enter Lil's Doughnut Shop. I also entered and bought four sugary doughnuts and coffee, and sat to eat them. I ate one and said loudly to the man next to me, "Wow, why did I buy all these? Can't eat another bite. Like some doughnuts, Sir?"

The stranger politely declined, but the deputy took the bait. "I'll take you up on that, Bub, if you don't want 'em, we don't want to waste nothin' so tasty as those."

"Of course, please take 'em. Pleased to meet ya. I'm Wyatt Earp, just in from Dodge City," I said casually.

"Sam Spence. How are ya? You work on a ranch, do ya?"

"Yep, wrangler, Bar X spread. Don't squeeze m'hand too hard, Deputy. Sore. I had to subdue a knife-wielding attacker-broke his jaw for 'im. Tough town, Dodge."

I stood up and hefted my .44 and stretched my fingers. "Spence, where can a fella practice a little shootin' around here?"

"Heck, Wyatt, let's just go to that field right over there." Spence pointed across the street and we ambled over there.

I said, "I'll bet I can hit that tin can…wait, I cleaned my gun this morning and forgot to load up again!"

"What you need, .44's? I got plenty." He gave me a handful.

Spence drew and… "BLAM!" Plugged the can! I drew and… "BLAM! BLAM! BLAM!" Wild. "Can't shoot because of my sore hand, Spence!"

Or because I never shot a gun before. Now I had some ammo. Wyatt would never walk around with an empty gun, now would he?

****

I was behind the counter at the library when I spotted the unruly patron- an old wizened guy reading "The Atlantic Monthly". He had strewn two cough drop wrappers onto the table!

I hastened to the scene. "Stranger, you'd best dispose of them wrappers in a proper way, <u>pronto</u>!"

I shifted my cheroot to the other side of my mouth and adjusted the .44 in my holster. "You ain't one of them Clantons are you? Plenty of room at the Dodge City Jail for those that flout the law!"

Well, I cowed him pretty good. Neat table again.

Gramps left and a little old lady with a knitted shawl came to the desk. She had an overdue book! Another renegade!

"Ma'am, I must inform you that this library has <u>rules</u>- and we give no quarter to no-accounts who return books <u>late</u>!"

"See that date on that slip? I'll underline it for you." I slammed my Bowie Knife into the wooden counter. "THUD!" It neatly underlined the date with the blade. Kind of hurt my hand on the hilt, but I didn't let on.

"Ayeeeeh!" said the little shawl lady, as she dropped her books and glasses on the floor on her way out the door.

"Ma'am! You can't leave them books on the floor like that! Come back here!"

Ms. Schnozzletwittle came out from the back room. "What all's going on out here?"

"Oh, nothin'. Just maintaining library order and rules."

This ZPA business was really paying off! The Wyatt Earp personality was great stuff! I might get a deputy job of some sort. I'll have to talk to that fella Spence, see how he got his good lawman position.

****

The next day Lucy came by the library. "What's with the cowboy duds?"

"Wyatt Earp. See, at the ZPA, I drew this card, so it's my trial personality, and it's really..."

"Really wacko stupid! It doesn't fit you at all, Iggy! Draw another card!"

"...really wacko stupid, and I think I'll get out of these clothes right now. I'll go back to my place and change!"

Lucy said, "I started to tell you the other day, I'm here in town to visit some members of the Crazy Chicken Behavioral Institute. They want to show off their figure-skating chicken and another one that sorts cashews with her beak... commercial potential, they say, but probably the ASPCA will get after them.

"Iggy, I have to visit these chicken people, the Hadleys, but my old car stopped working. Can you give me a ride and come

296

along to visit, too?"

"Of course, Lucy! I just happen to have a wonderful vehicle that can travel in the deep woods where there are no roads, even up steep hillsides!" I said.

"No, not deep woods, just roads, a few miles from here."

She came outside and looked over my ant-car. What a beauty it was, black shiny ant body, room for two like a sports car.

"Iggy, you are a complete idiot, aren't you? You expect me to get in that thing? It looks like a McCormick Reaper, Model 0.

But, my angel, Lucy, bless her heart, slowly climbed over the side of the black ant body. "Iggy, I don't want anybody to see me riding in this clown contraption!"

"Not to worry, we can't go on the roads legally, have to go across fields."

The ride was kind of jouncy, a drawback. After all, no wheels, fast-moving legs. A few gobs of mud flying up at you, ha, ha, ha. First stop was my rooming house, where I changed, shedding my blossoming personality and returning to being just Mr. Bland.

We started for the Hadley's house. Jounced some. "Wh - at D-do you th - ink-k, Lu - cy? Fu - n, hu - h?"

Mostly we went over nice easy fields and woods. Heading through a woodsy area we came across a peculiar vehicle. It was a cigar-shaped canvas blimp about six feet in diameter and it had long caterpillar treads from nose to tail, two underneath and at the sides. Holy Mackerel! Each tread had foot-long curved claws!

"Lucy, it's a vehicle, windows all around, a door. This thing claws its way through brush!"

"Curiosity KILLED the cat!" boomed a large man in a silvery suit that looked like Flash Gordon's Casual Friday outfit. I jumped a foot, the way you do when a large silvery man yells at you from behind.

"I see you kids like to snoop, that's what I think."

"Oh, Henry, leave them alone. I told you we were too close to town to come down," said Silvery Man's female companion (matching silver outfit).

"What my gruff husband means is it would be nice if you would just forget you saw us here. We like to keep a low profile. These 'Tree-top Torpedoes' were used to study the tree-top dwellers like birds and squirrels and a group formed with that in mind. Well, some us kind of got tired of stupid squirrels (sky-rats) and drifted away from that, but we like cruising around the tree-tops."

"She didn't mention she shoots the little $#&^*%& 's with her .38 when she gets a chance, hah!" said her tattletale husband.

"We're retired and some would say deranged. We can go all over the forested U.S. with no concern for roads, and in fact, it's pretty convenient not having any address, so no property taxes. And plenty of free walnuts and apples if you know where to go.

"The group got started when we did a few little jokes, like the Bigfoot tracks, the Jonestown Ghosts, the bikes floating up to rooftops. A little competition to see who could get the biggest newspaper write-up!"

"Gloria, you're blabbing too much!"

"Oh, don't be such a stick-in-the-mud, Henry. Where's your hospitality? C'mon, kids, we'll show you how our tree rover runs."

We climbed into the big spiky cigar. It was kinda cramped, and they clawed forward through ground-level brush and vines upwards to about 40 feet high. Kind of scary, really.

They used GPS to navigate, and special maps showing the forested areas.

"We'll show you some picnic fishing!" said Gloria. We clawed our way over the tree-tops with the motorized tread-claws to a wooded campground. Whew! Lotsa campfire smoke. We stopped directly over a picnic table. We were 30 feet above it.

Nobody at the table. The picnickers were near a campfire. We looked down through windows in the Tree-top Torpedo's belly as Gloria lowered the grapple hook.

"Get both handles, Gloria, or it'll spill out!"

She nabbed it and as the grapples closed they released a nice note:

"Thanks for the contribution! Sincerely, Your Friendly Park

Rangers"

The unhappy campers saw their basket being plucked up and they shouted ineffectual protests as we made a speedy retreat, claws whirling, leaves flying.

"Heck, Gloria, let's go straight across this valley, show 'em our waterfall picnic area. Government land, but what they don't know won't hurt 'em!"

We proceeded a few miles and crossed over some security fences.

"Hey, look at that shiny flying saucer down there," Gloria said.

We gawked out the windows, and sure enough through the heavy tree growth we could see a large disk. Gloria dipped lower and found underbrush so we went to the ground, and got out and walked around.

"We're going to get in big trouble," I said.

"Shhhhhh!" Lucy said. "There's a uniformed guy in a hammock... we're in some government facility, let's get out!"

"AHHHCHOOOO!" I sneezed and woke up the old guy!

"Who's there?" he said. "Must've dozed off. Hey, what're you doing here, anyway?"

"We just dropped by to see your big flying saucer."

"Oh, yeah, it's a beauty. I polish it all the time- one of my jobs- Bright's 99 works best. White-glove inspection every month y'know."

"Where's it from?"

"Hah! The great beyond! Been here since '47, and so have I."

Old-timer was very interested in the Tree-top Torpedo and of course, Gloria offered to demonstrate the many-clawed marvel. Lucy and I stayed behind to look at the saucer. Shiny metal, like chrome, about thirty feet in diameter with windows.

They returned and Elmer, the faithful saucer guard, was all excited about the tree vehicle.

"Wowsa! That's some tree climber. Where can I get one of those? I'd go all over the place."

There was some discussion all about the used TT market, the time of year for best deals, how to spot a cream puff, etc.

"Want to meet BLXPT! and SPRK!?" Elmer asked. "They're the crew. They landed in '47 and the Air Force guys have kept them here ever since. Ain't right y'know. They said they don't know what to do about all this space aliens arriving thing. Congressional committee comes every two years or so, but same old thing, a secret report. Don't tell nobody, OK?"

He went inside the building and came out with two short midgets that looked like Mickey Rooney if he were a big boxing glove.

"How are you, Little Buddy?" I said to one of 'em as I shook his claw.

"BLXPT!" he said. "SPRK!" his cohort said.

"This is BLXPT! and this is SPRK!" Elmer said.

"They've been trying to fix their ship since they got here, but it's pretty tough. How ya gonna get parts? Friendly, but communication is hard. And the only thing they'll eat is Twinkies. That and Moxie soda pop.

"I did teach these guys to play poker. They ain't so good at it, though, for smart aliens. They owe me a bundle. 'Course it's all IOU's 'cause they got no money, unless you want those square coins they got.

"Hey, look, they want to go into your tree climber! I don't blame 'em, do you?"

Then old Elmer suddenly said, "Let's all get out of here! I'm sick of polishin' that tin top! I want to be a tree hobo like you guys!"

There was not a lot of room, but the midgets were small, so away we twirled through the leafy tree-tops, until we got back to little ole DELETED. We retrieved my trusty ant-car on the way and I took our new friends BLXPT! and SPRK! to the library. They can be squatters in the storeroom, I was thinking.

Elmer headed off through the trees with Gloria and Henry.

Lucy said, "I'll pick up some Twinkies and Moxie for them, and bring it tomorrow, OK?"

****

The next day BLXPT! and SPRK! were still there, so either they liked the library or couldn't work the doorknobs with their claws. They had eaten parts of some books, but apparently didn't like them.

Ms. Schnozzletwittle came to work and wondered about the aliens.

"Ms. S., they followed me home and maybe we should adopt them at the library, what do you think? They can help out around here, plenty of sweeping up, book shelving…"

"Iggy, you are crazy, aren't you? Are these midgets from a circus? Why do they have claws for hands?"

"Ms. Schnozzletwittle, I'm surprised at you, at your lack of sympathy for those less fortunate than…."

Lucy appeared, looking worried. She took me aside and whispered.

"Iggy, I think we have to get out of here before the Feds show up and ask questions about these little guys and entering secret government facilities and stuff! What do you think?"

"Hmmm, maybe you're right, Lucy." We made a hasty exit, ignoring poor Ms. Schnozzletwittle's complaints about the uninvited guests.

I said, "Let's make tracks in my ant-car!" Would Ms. Perfect Dream Girl go with me?

"Iggy, thank you, but you know I can't stand that herky-jerky thing. Saphead's headed for California and I'm hitching a ride.

Did you know he writes children's stories? I was surprised. How'd you make out at your last ZPA meeting, by the way?"

"I drew the 'Elroy Dentroone' personality card. But I never heard of him."

"Good luck, Elroy." She gave me a hug. "Seeya!"

"Bye Lucy." I put the ant-car in gear and dashed for the deep woods.

That fink, Saphead Psmith! Did he have a scar? Oh yeah, above his right eye. What color were his eyes? Oh yeah, green...

About the Author

Joel Clark is an out-of-work engineer/software guy with no job prospects and thus is in default retirement status. He sometimes mows his small lawn, but mostly piddles around with amusing projects like vortex generators, aerial photography gimmicks, integraphs, and stories. He lives in Bloomfield, CT, but would consider relocating if a lucrative movie deal came up.

Made in the USA
Charleston, SC
06 December 2012